C000198716

MORE
BLACK
COUNTRY
CHAPELS

NED WILLIAMS

SUTTON PUBLISHING

Sutton Publishing Limited
Phoenix Mill · Thrupp · Stroud
Gloucestershire · GL5 2BU

First published 2006

Title page photograph: Sunday school
children celebrate an 'anniversary' at the
Mission in Pitt Street, West Bromwich.
(*Ribbon Mission archives*)

British Library Cataloguing in Publication Data
A catalogue record for this book is available from the
British Library.

ISBN 0-7509-4183-9

Typeset in 10.5/13.5 Photina.
Typesetting and origination by
Sutton Publishing Limited.
Printed and bound in England by
J.H. Haynes & Co. Ltd, Sparkford.

THE BLACK COUNTRY SOCIETY

The Black Country Society is proud to be associated with **Sutton Publishing** of Stroud. In 1994 the society was invited by Sutton Publishing to collaborate in what has proved to be a highly successful publishing partnership, namely the extension of the ***Britain in Old Photographs*** series into the Black Country. In this joint venture the Black Country Society has played an important role in establishing and developing a major contribution to the region's photographic archives by encouraging society members to compile books of photographs of the area or town in which they live.

The first book in the Black Country series was *Wednesbury in Old Photographs* by Ian Bott, launched by Lord Archer of Sandwell in November 1994. Since then almost 70 Black Country titles have been published. The total number of photographs contained in these books is in excess of 13,000, suggesting that the whole collection is probably the largest regional photographic survey of its type in any part of the country to date.

This voluntary society was founded in 1967 as a reaction to the trends of the late 1950s and early '60s. This was a time when the reorganisation of local government was seen as a threat to the identity of individual communities and when, in the name of progress and modernisation, the industrial heritage of the Black Country was in danger of being swept away.

The general aims of the society are to stimulate interest in the past, present and future of the Black Country, and to secure at regional and national levels an accurate understanding and portrayal of what constitutes the Black Country and, wherever possible, to encourage and facilitate the preservation of the Black Country's heritage.

The society, which now has over 2,500 members worldwide, organises a yearly programme of activities. There are six venues in the Black Country where evening meetings are held on a monthly basis from September to April. In the summer months, there are fortnightly guided evening walks in the Black Country and its green borderland, and there is also a full programme of excursions further afield by car. Details of all these activities are to be found on the society's website, **www.blackcountrysociety.co.uk**, and in *The Blackcountryman*, the quarterly magazine that is distributed to all members.

PO Box 71 · Kingswinford · West Midlands DY6 9YN

CONTENTS

YOUNG MEN'S BIBLE CLASS
PRIMITIVE METHODIST CHURCH,
Vicar Street, Dudley.

This is to certify that *Leonard Frederick Snow*

has been received into the fellowship of the above Class and
enrolled as a member.

BERT BISSELL, President.

DENNIS BLOOMER, Secretary.

DANIEL HULSON } School Supers.
ERNEST MITCHELL }

JOSEPH B. BISSELL, Minister.

JULY 18th 1926

This certificate dates from 1916, when it was issued to the 16-year-old Leonard Snow, welcoming him to Bert Bissell's Young Men's Bible Class, at the Vicar Street Methodist Chapel in Dudley. His daughter treasures it today. *(Viv Turner) Below:* A small collection of Salvation Army paperwork – best seen in full Technicolor! The enthusiastic chapel-hunter is constantly surprised by the wealth of paperwork and memorabilia chapel-goers have preserved to safeguard treasured chapel memories. *(Robert Merrick)*

INTRODUCTION

While working on *Black Country Chapels* in 2004, it soon became plain that such a book could not be comprehensive – there had simply been too many chapels at one time or another in the Black Country to include them all. Therefore, while launching that book, I hoped I would be given the chance to carry on researching the subject for a sequel: *More Black Country Chapels*. No one will be surprised I still have to plead that the subject has not been dealt with comprehensively. In fact I am not sure how many volumes might eventually be needed!

In this book I have tried to tackle two problems. First, I have sought to include areas of the Black Country left out of the first book or under-represented (even so, important geographical areas – like Wednesbury and Walsall – are still neglected). Second, I have tried to show how some Black Country towns have a different chapel history from others. The smaller towns tend to provide one chapel of each denomination and maybe one or two independent ones. But the larger towns – represented in this book by Dudley and Wolverhampton – might have several chapels of each denomination, to counter the 'opposition' and colonise the growing suburbs.

The author will probably be lynched for omitting Quarry Bank for the second time – so let's repeat the formula! Here is Mount Pleasant Wesleyan Chapel doing the honours once again in the Introduction (see *Black Country Chapels*, page 9). A more detailed picture of chapels in Quarry Bank is to be found in books about that township. Meanwhile, sorry to the folks in Wednesbury, Walsall, Lye, and Darlaston! *(Ned Williams)*

In *Black Country Chapels* I described several themes that could be separated from the main 'gazetteer' approach of exploring Black Country towns chapel by chapel. These themes were bricks and mortar, anniversaries, banners, tin tabernacles, plus the question of defining 'missions' and 'mission halls'. I have not repeated these categories, but you will find my interest in such things as banners and the use of corrugated iron still influencing my choice of photographs. The final chapter is devoted both to vanished chapels and those in alternative use. The more one studies this phenomenon, the more one is haunted by vanished chapels, many of which have left little record of their existence.

This leads to the subject of closure. During 2004 and 2005 I have attended about one closure a month. And so, if chapels arouse your curiosity, now is the time to go and inspect them: don't leave it too long, or that interesting building you always wanted to visit may have gone. To the fervent Christian the mere disappearance of bricks and mortar is not important – religion is about spiritual matters, not architecture – but this book looks at the subject as part of our social and cultural history: taking the view that the man-made environment is of interest – and of concern. Please, therefore, forgive the book's worldly preoccupation with chapels, the attention given to the appearance of buildings, and the spectacle of all the human activities that go on in them.

Everyone is singing their heart out at the closure of Allen Rough Chapel on 27 February 2005. The Reverend Roger Moore is presiding over the service. (See *Black Country Chapels*, pages 39 and 40.) Note the miner's lamp font in the centre of the picture. (*Ned Williams*)

Do we care if chapels are demolished? The long-disused Gospel Hall in Oldbury was demolished in June 1983 to make way for a new road and subsequent redevelopment. Now who remembers it? And where are its records? *(Express & Star)*

As well as bricks and mortar, this survey of local chapels also records the memorabilia, artwork, and artefacts that contribute to a chapel's history. Everything from paperwork to pews, via souvenirs of anniversaries and Sunday school prizes. Local archives may collect some of the paperwork: but where does everything else go?

The meaning of the word 'chapel' was discussed in the introduction to *Black Country Chapels*, so there is no need to return to the subject here, save to point out that many people have abandoned the term in favour of 'church'. But even if we focus on dissenting, nonconforming, or independent places for Christian worship, there is still plenty of scope for wondering who to include and who to

Somebody thought of saving a lacquered papier mâché collecting plate from Wolverhampton's Congregational Chapel at Snow Hill, dated 1849. *(Lawson Cartwright)*

exclude. Despite the fact the Salvation Army does not meet in chapels (except where it shares one with another denomination) I think of them as part of the Protestant Nonconformist tradition, and so I have included them. But I have excluded Seventh-Day Adventists, Christian Scientists, Christadelphians, Mormons, and Jehovah's Witnesses. I find them all of interest – and am sure they contribute greatly to life in the Black Country – but I have to draw the line somewhere!

Similarly, I have paid limited attention to various apostolic and evangelical congregations: from Assemblies of God and Elim Pentecostals to Kingsway churches and 'Christian Centres'. I mention them now and then because they sometimes occupy buildings I feel are chapel-like, and often they have histories that connect with mainstream Nonconformists. It is important that their heritage is recorded too.

Ned Williams
January 2006

How could the Salvation Army be excluded? The band and songsters at Dudley, July 1968, with Lieutenant Colonel and Mrs Nicol Kirkwood and Brigadier E. Chandler, centre front row. (*Corps Archive*)

1 West Bromwich

All branches of Nonconformity have been well represented in West Bromwich, but many buildings associated with them have disappeared in recent years. To have a road named 'Old Meeting Street' is a good start, and West Bromwich's proximity to Wednesbury guaranteed a Methodist presence, as John Wesley's visits to that town became the stuff of local legend. West Bromwich is also associated with the home of Francis Asbury (1745–1816), the first bishop of the American Methodist Church. But that is another story . . .

Independent dissenters in the West Bromwich area traced their history right back to the Act of Uniformity of 1662 and the defection of the Reverend Richard Hilton from the parish church. In the aftermath of 1662 the origins of the 'Old Meeting' are not clear, but by the early 1700s a congregation was established with premises in which to meet. As in other cases, the building was destroyed in 1715, only to be rebuilt the following year. In 1839 the place of worship was rebuilt and took on the name 'Ebenezer', occupying a sizeable plot of land, formerly belonging to the Jesson family, at Oakwood. In 1875 John Blackham launched his PSA movement at this building, the 'Pleasant Sunday Afternoon' (See *Black Country Chapels*, page 17). The 'Ebenezer' is seen on the left of this postcard view, while the centre of the picture is occupied by a Sunday school building of 1906. *(W. Boyd collection)*

The congregation at the Ebenezer, Old Meeting Street, eventually vacated their historic home to join with other Congregationalists in the town, and in 1974 the premises were sold to the Hindu community. In this 2005 picture it can be seen that the magnificent brick and terracotta Sunday school building of 1906 still stands but the Hindu temple architecture of the Shree Krishna can be seen next door. *(Ned Williams)*

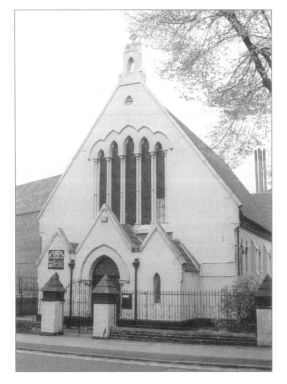

The voice of dissent raised at the Old Meeting House continued to be heard as Congregationalists, Baptists, and Unitarians established themselves. The 'Congs' built a chapel at Mayers Green in 1808. An offshoot of this was the Congregational chapel built in the High Street in 1879.

The Unitarians built this chapel in Lodge Road, which opened in April 1875. It was built in red brick and seated about 200 people. In this 2005 photograph, we can see the building has now been rendered, and is now occupied by the 'Mount Shilo' apostolic congregation. *(Ned Williams)*

This Edwardian postcard shows the Central Wesleyan Chapel in High Street, West Bromwich, just after the building had been refronted in 1905–6. The history of Wesleyan Methodism in West Bromwich goes back to John Wesley himself and his strong association with followers in Wednesbury. A Wesleyan chapel on this site first opened on 5 June 1835. This building was demolished in 1972 to make way for a large modern replacement, opened in 1974. Further Wesleyan chapels were opened at Swan Village, Spon Lane, Hill Top (part of a Wednesbury circuit), Beeches Road, Greets Green, Carters Green and the Lyng. *(W. Boyd collection)*

The Beeches Road Wesleyan Chapel was built in 1873, with Sunday school buildings added in 1906. Here, in 2005, it is owned by the Sikh community. *(Ned Williams)*

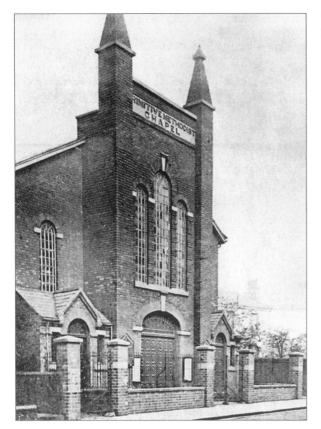

The Primitive Methodists arrived in West Bromwich from Darlaston, in a mission covering vast areas of the Black Country. This building in Queen Street was intended to be a public hall, but the 'Prims' took over and completed it as a chapel in 1847. It became the headquarters of the West Bromwich Primitive Methodist circuit. It closed in 1966. *(W. Boyd collection)*

Primitive Chapels quickly spread through West Bromwich: The Lyng and Guns Village in 1851, followed by Spon Lane a year later.

The Lyng Methodist Chapel of 1851 was replaced with this building, which opened on 30 September 1900. On 22 November 1940 it was hit by a German bomb, destroying the main part of the building rather than the tower. *(Ann Clarke collection)*

An architectural drawing by Cyril Moss of the Lyng Methodist Church, designed to replace the bomb-damaged building shown on the opposite page. It was built by J. & F. Wootton of Bloxwich, and was opened at 3 p.m. on 13 September 1952, when Cyril Moss handed the key to Mrs E.J. Crump, a senior member of the chapel. *(Ann Clarke)*

The brickwork of the 'new' Lyng Methodist Chapel can be glimpsed here in this Sunday school anniversary picture of about 1960. Betty Clarke, who contributed the photograph, is standing in the middle of the back row, while her son Alan is standing on the far left of the picture. Alan Clarke became the church organist. *(Ann Clarke)*

The 'old' Lyng Lane chapel was a Wesleyan outpost of 1880 vintage, built for £668 and seating 175 people – not to be confused with their Primitive Methodist rivals! It is not surprising this little chapel was too small for its own anniversaries. The 1954 anniversary is seen below, taking place at West Bromwich Town Hall, in the presence of the Mayor and Mayoress, Mr and Mrs Fisher. *(Sheila Wootton)*

2 West Bromwich & the Blue Ribbon Mission

In the West Bromwich Town Hall (opposite) a whole day of events and meetings was held on 1 August 1882 to launch a campaign on behalf of the Blue Ribbon Army. Francis Murphy – a passionate convert to the cause of Temperance – created the Blue Ribbon Army in America in 1877. Among his Black Country supporters was John Blackham of the Old Meeting House, West Bromwich.

The crusade had the effect of creating a permanent group of Temperance supporters in West Bromwich, who kept alive the 'Blue Ribbon' name. They looked for a site for a mission hall, and in November 1892 they laid the foundation stones of their hall in Pitt Street. They also established a Temperance Band.

What is not clear is how successfully the Blue Ribbon Army established itself elsewhere. References to the Blue Ribbon Army have also been found in Quarry Bank (where they also established a band) and Wordsley. The Temperance cause is usually more readily associated with the Band of Hope, and then the Salvation Army, which enjoyed success in the Black Country.

The West Bromwich Blue Ribbon Army Band in their new uniforms of the early 1930s, supplied by High Street tailors Morris & Dixon. The conductor was Thomas Russell and bandmaster Ephraim Edwards. *(Mission Archives)*

Having laid the foundation stone of a Blue Ribbon Gospel Mission Hall in Pitt Street, in 1892, the congregation built themselves a standard 'tin tabernacle' (see *Black Country Chapels*, pages 25–30). This picture was taken in 1969 when the congregation had to leave their corrugated iron gospel hall to seek another home. The Pitt Street premises were acquired by the Corporation prior to demolition work in the area, first stage in the redevelopment of the centre of West Bromwich. On the left is James Penn, who in 1961 had become only the third Superintendent of the Mission (preceded by James Lear and Joseph Lloyd). Note the poster advertising a visit from the Netherton Male Voice Choir from the People's Mission Hall in Swan Street. *(Mission Archives)*

What better backdrop can you have for a wedding photo than a tin tabernacle? Jeff Woodward marries May Paulton at the Gospel Blue Ribbon Mission in Pitt Street, West Bromwich. On either side of the minister stand Jim Holland and Joe Edwards – both future superintendents.

The interior of the Gospel Blue Ribbon Mission in Pitt Street, in which Jim Higginbottom occupies the pulpit after a children's crusade. Note the mission's banner, which still survives today.

On leaving Pitt Street, the Gospel Blue Ribbon Mission moved to the Grant Hall in Taylors Lane. It was an ex-dance hall purchased by the Corporation as a temporary home for the mission. The hall was dedicated on 25 November 1972, once it became clear their stay was likely to be permanent. Old foundation stones from Pitt Street have been let into the brickwork of the flanking wall. *(Ned Williams)*

Children, youth group members, and teachers hold up the Gospel Blue Ribbon Mission's old banner at the annual Flower Festival service on 10 July 2005. *(Ned Williams)*

3 Smethwick

Dissent and nonconformity came to the Smethwick area in 1810 when Congregationalists from Birmingham came to Cape Hill. Their High Street chapel in the centre of Smethwick was built in 1837, replacing an earlier building on the corner of Crockett's Lane. The chapel closed in 1961 and was purchased by members of the Sikh community. As the Guru Nanak Gurdwara it has been rebuilt and extended.

The three main Methodist denominations, Wesleyan, New Connexion and Primitive, were well represented in Smethwick, but the number of chapels has been much reduced by closures and amalgamations. A Baptist congregation was established in 1866 and found a home in Cross Street. The Smethwick Gospel Mission Hall has flown the flag of independence.

The imposing Regent Street Particular Baptist Chapel was built between 1877 and 1879. It replaced a chapel built in Cross Street in 1869. A Primitive Methodist chapel was built on the opposite side of the road in 1887, just around the corner, and closed in 1972. The Baptists have survived but have divided the building so that the place of worship is now on the first floor and the ground floor space can be put to other use. (Ned Williams)

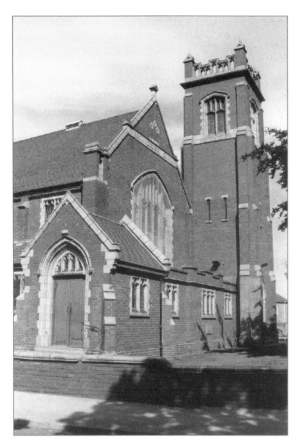

The Wesleyan Methodists out at New Street were not centrally located and the chapel has now been converted into a factory. It was replaced by the Elizabeth Akrill Memorial Church, Broomfield, which opened in 1931 – an impressive reworking of the style of chapels built in red brick and terracotta in the 1900s. *(Ned Williams)*

The architectural style is maintained in the adjoining Sunday school building. Both pictures were taken in 2005. *(Ned Williams)*

West Smethwick Methodist Chapel, opened on 10 March 1928. Designed by Messrs Webb and Gray, and built by J. Guest & Sons, it was an impressive replacement for Spon Lane Wesleyan Methodist Church (1841–1927) and St Paul's Road Wesleyan Chapel which was a 'tin tabernacle' building of 1904 vintage – occupying the site of the present youth hall.

The Baptists established a mission in the vast inter-war Londonderry Estate and completed this building in 1932. *(Ned Williams)*

The Smethwick Gospel Hall, at the Cape Hill end of Smethwick, was founded by John Farren. It was built on the site of a coffee-house and was rather grand compared with the halls usually used by 'Brethren' congregations. Construction began in 1901, as recorded by the date on the building, but was not officially opened until 15 March 1902. The front part of the building shown in the above drawing was sold to the Soho Co-operative Society in 1912. In its truncated form the hall survived until early 2005. *(From Keith Finney's Memoir in Colin Bellamy collection)*

'Focus', a gospel music group from the Smethwick Gospel Hall appearing at Netherton's Swan Street Mission Hall, December 2004. The group is led by Colin Bellamy, an elder of the Gospel Hall, seen standing in the centre next to Bill Cauldwell who is looking round from the organ console. *(Ned Williams)*

4 Oldbury & Langley

Oldbury grew into a large town dominated by heavy industry and therefore was home to a number of chapels – many of which have now disappeared. The area around Oldbury contained that fascinating Black Country mix of small villages, industrial settlements and areas in which agriculture survived for much of the nineteenth century. Chapel-hunters should not be deterred by the present suburban sprawl.

Left: Tipton Road Methodist Church, on the main road between Oldbury and Tipton, looks fairly modern to anyone gazing at it while waiting at the traffic lights. The small stone plaque in the gable reveals that this was a Wesleyan chapel dating back to 1839. *(Ned Williams) Right:* The 'Bethel' chapel in Broad Street, Langley Green, was awaiting demolition when this photograph was taken in the autumn of 2004. It was built in 1877 for the New Connexion Methodists, replacing an older building. *(Ned Williams)*

Brades Village on the road between Oldbury and Tipton was a typical semi-isolated industrial settlement of this area. Brades Steelworks, which made edge tools, was built by the canal, but the village grew up on the northern side of the turnpike road. St Matthew's Mission, facing Albion Street, was built in the centre of it. It was opened and dedicated on St Matthews Day, 21 September 1892, and was able to hold 165 people. *(Ken Rock collection)*

Rounds Green grew up on the other side of the works and the Primitive Methodists built this chapel in Brades Road in 1849, replacing it in 1904 with a chapel that lasted until 1962. *(Ken Rock collection)*

The Ebenezer Chapel in Hunt Street, Oldbury, was built by members of the congregation – begging materials as they did so. They belonged to the Wesleyan Reform Union and opened on 10 February 1875. *(Ken Rock collection)*

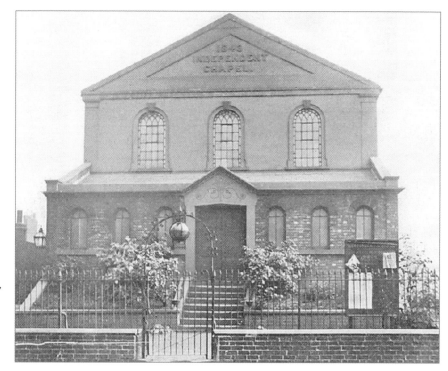

The Oldbury Independent Chapel, in Talbot Street, opened on 18 July 1843, and was enlarged in 1866. *(Ken Rock collection)*

The New Connexion Tabernacle in Tabernacle Street, Oldbury, first opened in 1838. It was largely rebuilt in 1870, with a large Sunday school built behind it, opening on 1 July 1870. It commanded a good position in central Oldbury but all this part of the town has disappeared as a result of modern developments. *(Ken Rock collection)*

The Wesleyan Methodist Chapel on the corner of Church Street and Wesley Street has survived in all its glory. It is now used by a Church of God congregation. It was opened on 25 October 1853 and accommodated 850 worshippers. It had cost £6,000 to build the chapel and Sunday school and was Oldbury's most ambitious Nonconformist project up to that time. It was renovated and 'improved' in the 1890s. *(Ned Williams)*

Langley Independent Chapel, 'Zion', Langley Green Road, as it was in 1900 when Henry McKean was compiling his book *Picturesque Oldbury*. (Henry was Minister at the Unitarian chapel in Birmingham Street, hence his interest in photographs of local chapels.) The congregation at Zion, and the buildings on this site, have a long and complicated history. The story begins in the late eighteenth century with a Moravian minister preaching under a tree in Langley, resulting in a first chapel being built in 1798. Here we see a Sunday school building of 1860 (on the right) and a chapel built in 1878 (on the left). *(Ken Rock collection)*

The building on the right (above) has been replaced with a caretaker's house in this 1905 picture in which the Sunday school celebrates its centenary. *(Sam Round)*

Zion Chapel's Sunday school and 'Band of Hope', Langley Green, probably taking part in a parade in Langley in 1911 to mark the coronation of King George V. The crowd includes Tom Fanthom (see page 30). *(Sam Round)*

The Zion Sunday school eventually outgrew the 1860 building and plans were made to replace it. Despite the First World War plans went ahead, and bricks were sold individually during 1915. The foundation stones (above) were laid early in 1916 and the school was completed by the autumn, opening on 1 October 1916. Seated between the bricks are (left to right) S. Jones, S. Cross, J. Hollinshead and R. Beighton. The new Sunday school building now dominates the chapel site. *(Sam Round)*

This 1990 picture of the Sunday school pupils shows the entrance now added to the 1916 building. The old chapel was replaced with a new 'sanctuary' built to the left of this entrance in 1977. *(Val Read collection)*

Sunday school anniversary service at Zion, Langley, on 26 June 2005 – using the stage in the 1916 Sunday school building. As 2005 is the 200th Anniversary of the Sunday school a special reunion anniversary event was planned for 16 July 2005. *(Ned Williams)*

Left: On 16 June 2005 Eric Fanthom came along to Zion's 200th Anniversary Sunday school reunion with his own display of photographs to add to the many on show. On the bottom right of the display is a picture of Thomas Fanthom, Eric's grandfather, who is commemorated by a plaque in the chapel. *Right:* The chapel celebrated its 200th Anniversary in 1990 – not to be confused with the Sunday school's bicentenary in 2005 – hence the two banners. *(Ned Williams)*

Sunday school-children and the Zion Sunday school's 2005 banner, on display at the reunion of 16 July. *(Ned Williams)*

Vast numbers turned up on 16 July 2005 for the Zion Sunday school bicentenary reunion in Langley on a sunny day. *(Ned Williams)*

To celebrate the bicentenary of the Zion Sunday the reunion on 16 July 2005 featured an exhibition of photographs and memorabilia, a medallion was struck and souvenir mugs were produced, a feast was laid on and someone baked a cake. Lesley Bowen and Vivian Robinson display the anniversary cake. *(Ned Williams)*

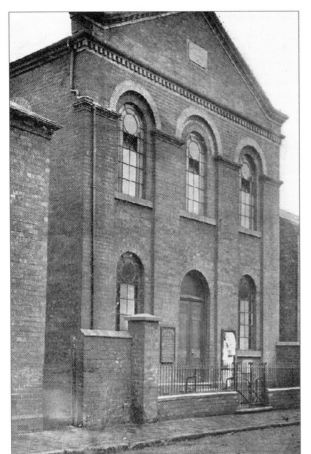

The Primitive Methodists first opened a chapel in Spring Street, Langley, in 1861, but it was replaced with this lofty building in 1872. *(Ken Rock)*

By 1950 the chapel was no longer being used and it was put up for sale. A local amateur dramatics company, the Oldbury Repertory Players, was looking for a home, and with a loan from Councillor Charles Barlow they were able to purchase the building for £1,700. It took five years to convert the former chapel into a theatre but it was opened in triumph on 10 January 1956 by Councillor Barlow's widow. It was improved in 1960, and again after a fire in 1972, but today, in 2005, the old chapel is still going strong as a theatre. The loftiness of the building provides an excellent raked auditorium. *(Ned Williams)*

The little chapel at Causeway Green was built in 1863 as the result of the dedication of one man – rather like 'Cope's Chapel' in Wolverhampton. Mr H. Parkes of Causeway Green became a Wesleyan Methodists and worshipped with great fervour and regularity at Warley Chapel. He purchased this site with a view to building a local chapel – but met with opposition within the circuit. He carried on at his own expense and won the day. The 2005 picture, below, shows how simply has been modernised. *(Ken Rock and Ned Williams)*

In the 1900s a group of young people from George Street Methodist Chapel, in Warley, came together to discuss religious and moral issues of the day. Eventually they rented the corner of a field adjoining Pound Lane and purchased a second-hand wooden building, formerly a photographic studio. In April 1906 the first meeting was held in this building of the 'Warley Institute'. *(Terry Daniels)*

From about 1912 they began to call themselves the 'Warley Institutional Church' (WIC) and by the time the First World War began they had collected enough bricks to start building something more church-like. However, construction did not begin until 1925, and after its completion these 'Oldbury Miners' (on strike) came to finish setting out the grounds in 1926. *(Terry Daniels)*

Soon after the opening of the Warley Institutional Church on 7 March 1925 this picture of church and congregation was taken. *(Terry Daniels)*

The building was designed by Frederick York and the foundation stones were laid in September 1924 to form the sill to the main window. Each stone reflected a core social or moral principle, and well-known people from far and wide came to lay them. The 'Social Justice' stone, for example, was laid by George Lansbury.

The congregation produced many people who became involved in local politics, education, or social welfare, and the church was identified with pacifist and socialist principles.

The Institute's first leader was George Norman Robbins, followed by Arthur Field: both local teachers. Terry Daniels, who has supplied these historic pictures, is only the third president of the WIC, and hopes to celebrate its centenary in 2006. *(Ned Williams)*

Although the Warley Institutional Church took more interest in politics and social issues than many others, there was still time for sporting and cultural activities. There was a large field behind the church and here, just before the First World War, we see the Tennis Club at rest. *(Terry Daniels)*

Sunday school anniversaries prevailed at the Warley Institutional Church just like any other, but the dress code wasn't, perhaps, as strict. This was 1958 and girls in the front row include Ann Law, Maureen Gould, Susan Porritt and Barbara Jones. The WIC still uses The Fellowship Hymn Book, which is unusual, but worship is in Methodist style. The WIC also currently shares its premises with the Salvation Army. *(Terry Daniels)*

5 The Road to Rowley

The road from Dudley to Blackheath runs along the western shoulder of the ridge that bisects the Black Country. At its highest point the road passes St Giles' Church – a reminder that one is in that least well-defined of all Black Country boroughs, Rowley Regis – sprawling from Old Hill and Cradley Heath in the west, across to Tividale on the eastern side of the divide. As one might expect, chapels along this axis serve small communities – starting with Knowle Methodist Church, which looks across from the ridge, into the heart of Netherton, to the tiny 'Church in the Garden', from which missionary tracts flew from Blackheath to remote corners of the Earth.

In the early 1860s New Connexion Methodists from Darby End climbed Springfield Lane and held open-air services and crusades on the sides of the Rowley Hills. A congregation was established in the Springfield/Knowle area, and land on the hillside was purchased in 1868. The chapel was completed a year later. A schoolroom was added in 1898 but both buildings suffered the effects of subsidence. The original chapel, built further up the hillside than this one, was replaced by this building at an opening ceremony on 25 September 1907. By this time the New Connexion had become the United Methodists (the original chapel remained in partial use for a short time).
This building was erected by H. Pugh & Sons of Old Hill at a cost of £1,550, and was designed by W.J. Cornwall. The original Sunday school building, standing to the right and rear of this building, although affected by subsidence, remained in use until 1952. A new Sunday school was built and opened in 1953. (Ned Williams)

The Rowley Regis Endowed School Mission has a long history, in which the threads of religious and secular education intertwine. Putting that behind us, the building seen here, in 2005, opened as a Sunday school and a church on 25 October 1925. The building had previously been the Britannia Works and it took a great deal of work to prepare it for chapel use. It was originally hidden from the High Street by two cottages, but these were demolished in 1935 and the mission acquired the land, which is now a car park. *(Ned Williams)*

Bare brick walls were clad in matchboard and heavy wooden beams were replaced with lighter trusses, and over the years much voluntary work has gone into improving the environment of the Endowed Mission, which still enjoys its independence today. *(Ned Williams)*

Not far from the Rowley Endowed Mission is 'The Church in the Garden' at No. 121 in the Ross. It was created by Walter Darby (1901–89), seen here by the front garden noticeboard, welcoming people to his undenominational chapel-like place of worship. *(Martin Pearson collection)*

Walter Darby had no wealth or education, being a manual worker in the iron trades all his working life. But in his early twenties he experienced a dramatic conversion, and having embraced Christianity, he wanted to become a minister. Discouraged by others, he decided to work independently from his garden shed. He became a formidable tract-writer, producer and distributor, and as others came to help him, a congregation was established that began to meet in one of his sheds. Here we see Walter surrounded by letters and papers, with his Adana printing press in the foreground, in about 1948. *(Martin Pearson collection)*

Regular meetings in the garden shed began in about 1944. A year or two later we find Walter, on the right, running a crusade helped by, left to right: Lawson Darby, Rose Dovey (still a member of the congregation today), Arthur Adams, Hilda Hill, David Hill, Ernie Hodgetts and Albert Homer. *(Martin Pearson collection)*

Walter distributed tracts, from his base in the Ross, on behalf of the Homeland Missionary Society, seen here in the 1930s, before establishing the Church in the Garden. Back row, left to right: Albert Williams, Ron Shaw, Albert Homer, Ben Hill and Ernie Hodgetts. Front row: James Parkes, Walter Darby, Pastor Whittle, Joe Shepherd and Brian Homer. *(Martin Pearson collection)*

Using one shed as his office, Walter converted a greenhouse to a church. The structure went through several modifications, extensions, and rebuilds, culminating with the acquisition of a brick-built entrance. Complete with organ and pulpit, the building was able to accommodate up to thirty worshippers.

When Walter Darby died in October 1988, his thirty-year-old grandson, Martin Pearson, came to live in the house and take over the running of 'The Church in the Garden'. *(Martin Pearson collection)*

Martin Pearson ultimately felt that his grandfather's old green shed-like church was wearing out. In November 1990 permission was obtained from the local council to build a new church behind the old one. It was completed by 1 December 1991. The following year work began to demolish the old building, in the foreground, and clear up the garden approach to the new church. *(Martin Pearson's collection)*

The Birmingham Road Methodist Chapel, built where Rowley's Birmingham Road enters Blackheath, had its origins in a New Connexion society that first met in a cottage in Yew Tree Lane in 1840. Later the congregation moved to Siviters Lane. Then this large church-like building was constructed on Birmingham Road. It opened on 23 October 1906, having cost £8,000 to complete. The brick and terracotta style makes it similar to Old Hill's Wesleyan Chapel of 1904, and Blackheath's High Street Methodist Church of 1902.

In 1987 the Sunday school building behind the chapel was sold and the money ploughed into modernising the rest of the premises, which reopened on 21 March 1987.

In 1996 the Methodist Churches of Blackheath amalgamated, meeting at Birmingham Road until the new 'Central' premises were ready. This building reopened as the Kingsway International Church on 24 April 2005. *(Ned Williams)*

Blackheath Salvation Army Band outside their hall in Park Street, only a few yards from the Bible Hall seen below. *(Anthony Page)*

The Blackheath Bible Hall, seen here in 2005 awaiting demolition, never won any prizes for outstanding architecture, but buildings like this in the Black Country always have an interesting tale to tell. *(Ned Williams)*

The Blackheath Bible Hall was created by Llewellen Walker and Arthur Nock (seen below, second from right in his trilby). The original building, seen above, was a wooden structure opened in 1924. In the early 1960s it was demolished and they moved into the brick building next door in Park Street, seen on the previous page. Arthur Nock had died in 1954 and the running of the hall passed to his son. The final service was held in January 2003 and it was demolished in 2005. Although independent all its life, the hall was visited by American evangelists, some of whom are seen sitting in the front row in the picture below. It is believed that Arthur Nock was initially converted by an American evangelist visiting Old Hill in the 1920s. It is interesting that such events led both Arthur Nock and Walter Darby to establish small independent 'chapels' in the Rowley area. *(Enid Bridgwater)*

6 Halesowen

The town of Halesowen is still dominated by its historic church, but in the nineteenth century it was nicely surrounded by chapels, some of which have disappeared, others acquiring secular use. St John's Church had a dissenting vicar during the 1650s, but the forces of dissent and nonconformity took some time to establish themselves in the town.

In 1804 independent meetings were held in a barn and this group of Congregationalists managed in 1811 to build a fine chapel on the corner of Hagley Street and Cornbow. It occupied this prominent town-centre site until 1960, when it was demolished to make way for the regeneration of Halesowen's town centre. Meanwhile, in 1909, the Congregationalists built a Sunday school on land in Hagley Road. It was a handsome building designed by local architect, A.T. Butler. After the closure and demolition of their chapel of 1811, the Congregationalists were able to build a new chapel in front of the Sunday school, and this is the construction that faces us today as we turn into Hagley Road.

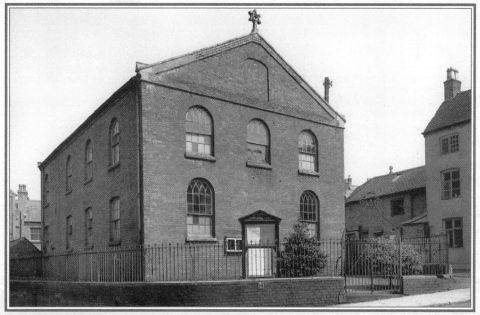

The 1811 Congregational Chapel on the corner of Hagley Street and Cornbow.
The decision to build this chapel was taken in 1807. By the time of its 150th Jubilee in 1957 it was facing closure. After closure the organ was stored, then rebuilt in the present church. The cross from the apex of the gable was larger than everyone had imagined and defied preservation. *(David Eades)*

The new chapel was built in front of the 1909 Sunday school building on the corner of Hagley Road, and was opened on 8 July 1961. The Congregationalists became the United Reformed Church in 1972, joined in 1984 by the Methodists from Birmingham Street. Since then it has been the Halesowen United Church. *(Ned Williams)*

Methodism seems to have been established in Halesowen by 1825, and the congregation became part of the New Connexion. In December 1842 they opened this chapel: 'Zion', in Stourbridge Road. Zion closed in 1979 but the building was then leased to the Zion Pentecostal Church, which later moved to the former Webb Ivory factory in Little Cornbow. The old Zion, seen here in 2004, is now home to a suite of offices, known as Church Court. *(Ned Williams)*

The Primitive Methodists were successful in the Halesowen area, and opened their first chapel at Hasbury in 1837, a second in Birmingham Street following in 1848. This building followed twenty years later. A foundation stone was laid in 1868 by Sir Benjamin Hingley, one time MP for Halesowen, and the building is now used as a restaurant, trading as 'Benjamin's'. The congregation left in 1984 to join the Congregationalists at Hagley Road. *(Joan Price)*

The choir at Birmingham Street Methodist Chapel in one of the galleries that now form such a striking part of the restaurant! Third and fourth from right are Eric and Joan Price, respectively, who supplied the photograph. *(Joan Price)*

The Baptists in Halesowen eventually built a chapel in Stourbridge Road, almost next door to the Primitive Methodists, in 1878. It was much enlarged in 1899, and a Sunday school was built alongside. The main chapel building was sold in the 1980s to Eric Emery, who had also bought the Methodist chapel. The former chapel is now Hales Court (offices) and the Baptists now meet in the ex-Sunday school on the left. *(Ned Williams)*

Halesowen Baptists photographed after their carol service of 19 December 2004 in the former Sunday school, which is now their place of worship. Seated fourth from left is David Trace, one time minister, and behind the lectern in the back row is David Umbers, the present minister. *(Ned Williams)*

Following their success in Hasbury and then Birmingham Street, the Primitive Methodists built further chapels in the Halesowen area: at Short Cross in 1868, at Hayseech in 1870 (see *Black Country Chapels*), and Shenstone in 1894. The above photograph was taken in 1978. *(David Eades)*

The Primitive Methodists purchased land at Short Cross in 1867 and a schoolroom was erected. A chapel followed in 1891, sited to the left of the chapel seen above. The interior of this second building is seen on the right, *c.* 1930.

The 1891 chapel then became a schoolroom (demolished in 1976), when a new chapel was built in 1934. The latter was designed by Stanley Beach, built by J.M. Tate & Son, and opened on 31 January 1935. The organ, communion rail, and table, plus a window, were transferred from the 1891 building. The 1935 frontage, as seen above, has now been altered with the addition, in 2004, of a porch. *(Irene Brittain)*

The 2nd Halesowen Company of the Boys Brigade (North Worcs. & Dudley Battalion), photographed outside Short Cross Chapel in 1967. The company was established at the end of the 1950s by Jim Price, with the help of Brigaders from the Overend Mission. A Girls' Brigade company (1st Halesowen) followed in the early 1960s, led by Pat Oliver. *(Irene Brittain)*

This modest little building on the Hagley Road is the Bethel Mission Church, with a history stretching back to 1926. It was started by young men from the Stourbridge Road Baptist Chapel, who were also members of the Halesowen Athletic Club. They split up, and a faction led by W.J. Carter started meeting as a Sunday afternoon 'men's class' at the Conservative Club in Great Cornbow. It expanded and in 1939 acquired this site in Hasbury. *(Ned Williams)*

When the Bethel Mission moved to Hasbury they occupied a wooden building, which had been a First World War structure transferred to Hasbury from Longbridge. It is seen here as background to a 1963 wedding photograph, when Brenda Dubber married Frank Foulkes. As activities at the Bethel expanded, the building deteriorated, and in 1966 the decision was made to replace it, using volunteer labour and a concrete 'Marley' building. The new mission was opened on 27 November 1971. The interior of the new building is seen below in 2000 – the table came from Belle Vale Chapel. (*Richard Westwood*)

Opening the new mission in 1971 was not the end of the story. At the 50th Anniversary in 1976 it was decided to erect a new brick-built hall at the rear of the mission. Once again it was constructed by volunteers, and was not completed until 1984. Mary Ward (left), a member of the congregation, opens the new hall in 1984, and receives a presentation from Richard Westward, the Bethel's most recent leader. *(Richard Westwood collection)*

Back in 1957 we see a typical anniversary scene at the Bethel, with everyone on a platform in front of the partition that separated chapel from Sunday school in the old wooden building. On the left, Fred Taylor, who was pastor at the time. *(Richard Westwood collection)*

7 Old Hill

The Wesleyans and the Baptists at Spring Meadow earned a mention on page 138 of *Black Country Chapels*, and the Macefield Mission was glimpsed on pages 37 and 38. And so we return to Old Hill to look at two other chapels: the Ebenezer in Station Road, and St James's, now in Highgate Street, but once dominating the landscape at 'the Cross'.

This picture, taken in 1987 by congregation member Brian Pegg, captures the way in which St James's dominated Old Hill Cross. It was sometimes known locally as 'The Little Chapel' or 'The Rhubarb'.
It was built in 1876 and was part of the Independent Wesleyan Reform Union: a group that had broken away from the mainstream Wesleyans in 1849. The Sunday school building on the right was opened on 17 May 1909.
The Chapel was served with a Compulsory Purchase Order in May 1986, to make way for the Old Hill Bypass. The last service in this building was held on 20 September 1987, and for two and a half years worship took place in temporary premises at Highgate Street, until a new chapel could be built on that site. (*Brian Pegg*)

The interior of St James's, Old Hill Cross, photographed from the balcony in 1986, when it was known the building faced demolition. *(Brian Pegg)*

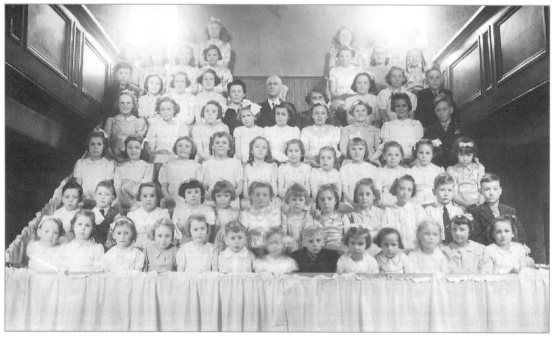

An anniversary scene at St James's, *c.* 1966. Gladys Gill, the lady sitting next to the gentleman in the centre of the picture, became a trustee and stalwart of the chapel, later opening the new building in Highgate Street. *(Ruth Pritchard)*

The traditional stone-laying ceremony took place in Highgate Street, Old Hill, on 22 April 1989, for a new St James's Chapel. The stone was laid by Clarence Dunn, aged eighty-six, who was the oldest member of the congregation. On the left, he is watched by the Reverend E.J.E. Small and Mr Harper, representing the contractors. The foundation stone was incorporated into a wall that is now inside the entrance to the building. *(Ruth Pritchard collection)*

The new St James's, Old Hill, seen here in 2005, was opened on Saturday 17 March 1990 by Mrs Gladys Gill, trustee and lifelong member of the congregation, and was dedicated 'To the Glory of God' by the minister, the Reverend E.J.E. Small. *(Ned Williams)*

A social gathering, probably during the Second World War, held in the old Sunday school building that had been adjacent to the chapel at Old Hill Cross. *(Ruth Pritchard collection)*

The congregation at St James's Old Hill, Highgate Street, after the anniversary service held on 20 March 2005. *(Ned Williams)*

The St James's, Old Hill, Ladies' Meeting, photographed during the 1930s. Miriam Powis, on the left, front row, is a member of the Ladies' Meeting today. Note that many of them are wearing white ribbons on their lapels. The 'Little White Ribboners' was yet another Temperance organisation, as seen by Miriam's card reproduced below. The location was a Temperance Meeting held at the home of one of the Woodhouses in Barrs Road (see *Black Country Chapels*, page 12). *(Miriam Golden)*

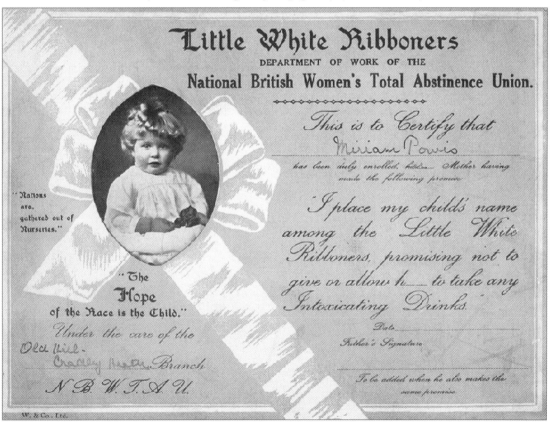

The Ebenezer Baptist Chapel in Station Road, Old Hill, is an impressive example of chapel architecture, beautifully built in a strong red brick.

The Ebenezer Baptist congregation was a breakaway group from the Spring Meadow Chapel, which formed in October 1902. As a group of Strict Baptists, they first rented a room in the local Board school. In 1903 they acquired the land in Station Road, and on 7 September 1903 the foundation stones of this building were laid. The opening services were held on 28 April 1904. *(Ned Williams)*

 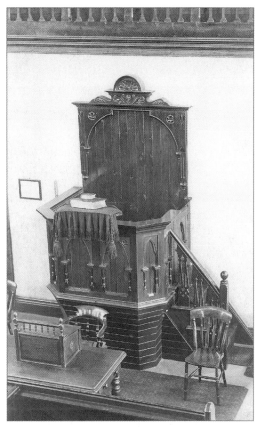

Left: Mr J. Calcott, Ebenezer's first minister, came to the chapel in January 1910. He combined the Ministry with running a large motor manufacturing company in Coventry until his death in 1924. *Right:* The pulpit at Ebenezer, which is still in use today, as can be seen in the picture below, taken at an anniversary service on 23 April 2005, with Mr Roland Burrows in the pulpit. *(Ned Williams)*

An attempt to line up the entire congregation of Ebenezer Chapel, Old Hill, on 20 September 2003, to mark the centenary of laying the foundation stones. *(Roland Burrows collection)*

Back to St James's, Old Hill: Major Ray Baddams of the Salvation Army, Sue Haggart (secretary and trustee), and Ann Underhill (preachers' secretary) in front of the Sunday school banner at the anniversary service held on 20 March 2005.

The Salvation Army Corps from Cradley Heath (see *Black Country Chapels*, page 141) have been homeless since August 2004. They have temporary use of St James's, Old Hill, and the Four Ways Baptist chapel in Cradley Heath. *(Ned Williams)*

8 Beyond Netherton

A large chapter was devoted to the chapels of Netherton in *Black Country Chapels* but even so, several managed to get left out! Two independent chapels deserve attention, as well as the Methodists at Dudley Wood.

On the outskirts of Netherton the new Sledmere Estate was built in the mid-1950s, and several members of the Peoples Mission, Swan Street (see *Black Country Chapels*, page 101), felt they should provide something for the residents. They began by holding a tent-based crusade (see above), in which evangelist Adam Chambers led the proceedings. By 1959 they were able to build the Emmanuel Church (right). Although the chapel was damaged by fire in 2005, this independent congregation carries on its work. *(Trevor Lowe)*

The Wesley Bible Institute in Cole Street, Darby End, also maintains its independence in the twenty-first century. This began as a breakaway from the nearby Wesleyan chapel just before the First World War. The congregation can be seen building their 'Institute' in the picture above. Below, we see the building completed in 1915. It became a sanctuary to young men affected by unemployment in the 1920s and fielded a very strong football team! *(Betty Nash)*

Left: The Bible Institute also managed to afford a professionally made banner, probably the work of George Tuthill (see *Black Country Chapels*, page 19). *(Betty Nash)*

Dudley Wood Wesleyan Methodist Chapel on opening day, 23 October 1907. This attractive red brick and terracotta building was a replacement for an earlier building, which had been affected by subsidence. *(Fred & Winnie Emery)*

Foundation stones are laid, and sometimes relaid, in the history of a chapel. Miss Olwen Bytheway does the honours on this occasion, watched by the Reverend Arthur Page. The inscription on the stone reads: 'This is the original stone from the previous Sunday school erected in 1866, and relaid by the scholars – 19th September 1960.' *(Fred & Winnie Emery)*

Dudley Wood Methodist Chapel, Dudley Wood Road, Netherton, 1980s. This chapel was opposite the Cradley Heath Speedway Stadium, and does enjoy a proximity to Cradley Heath – but it is definitely in Netherton! *(Jeff Parkes)*

On 8 May 2005 the congregation held their last service in the main chapel building at Dudley Wood. The building was then put on the market to be sold for redevelopment. The congregation consequently moved into the Sunday school building. *(Ned Williams)*

9 Stourbridge

Stourbridge has 'something for everybody': from Anglican and Roman Catholic churches to a modern 'Christian Community' church, where Christianity is mixed with the ideas of Rudolf Steiner. Early dissenters are represented by a Quaker Meeting House, well worth a visit, dating back to about 1688.

Dissenters built a chapel in 1698, pulled down in 1715 and later replaced. By the end of the eighteenth century the Baptists were meeting in Stourbridge, and are represented at Hanbury Hill today. The Wesleyan, New Connexion, and Primitive Methodists all established themselves relatively close to the town centre, nurturing congregations in the suburbs. For example, Mission Halls were built at Norton and at Chawn Hill.

Stourbridge Unitarian Chapel, Lower High Street, photographed in 2005 and looking rather forlorn. When the independent dissenters split in 1788 this formerly Presbyterian congregation adopted Unitarianism, occupying this chapel in Lower High Street. It was rebuilt in 1861 and the Sunday school building glimpsed on the right was added later. For many years it stood opposite the Congregational chapel, which closed in 1978, the congregation migrating to St John's Church, near the bus station. *(Ned Williams)*

It seems John Wesley made only one visit to Stourbridge on 19 March 1770: yet twenty years later a Methodist community was in existence. At one stage the congregation met in a theatre, located, aptly, in Theatre Road. It was ministers from Dudley who took the first steps towards erecting a Wesleyan chapel in New Road. This opened in 1805, as clearly stated on the exterior of the building. In 1828 the New Road Chapel left the Dudley circuit to lead a new Stourbridge circuit. A Sunday school building was added in 1866. Soon after the First World War the congregation began planning a replacement and accumulating a 'Building Fund'.

A valedictory service was held on 1 May 1927, and on 8 September the foundation stone for the new church was laid. *(Fran Davis)*

A contemporary drawing of the new church in New Road, completed for 28 June 1928. The architects were Messrs Crouch, Butler, and Savage. The builders were S. Swift & Son. It makes an interesting comparison with the church built for the Methodists at Beckminster (Wolverhampton) two years earlier, and is equally 'church-like'. *(Fran Davis)*

A 1950s postcard shows a Midland Red bus traversing a quiet and leafy version of New Road, before the present ring-road was thought of. The proximity of the catholic church and the Methodist church is also apparent. *(200th Anniversary Exhibition)*

New Road features again in this picture of a parade risking life and limb as the ring-road traffic races by in the 1980s. The 12th Stourbridge Guide and Brownie Company are based at New Road.

The 12th Stourbridge Brownies at New Road in 1993. *(200th Anniversary Exhibition, collected by Fran Davis)*

The church-like interior of the New Road building, decorated for the 1805–2005 bicentenary. It is planned to put in a new floor roughly at the level of the top of the columns, to create more space for community use. *(Ned Williams)*

A New Road anniversary group on 22 May 2005. Left to right: John Clift, Mike Evanson, Janet Clift, Robin Baggott, Fran Davis, Dave Cormell, Pam Cooke, Helen Tromans, Tina Gittings, Sue Carless, Michael Carless (organist), Dot Bagley, Pauline Leary, and John Thomas. The Reverend Peter Clarke reluctantly occupies the pulpit. *(Ned Williams)*

Cast of a New Road pantomime of 1954. *(New Road 200th Anniversary Collection)*

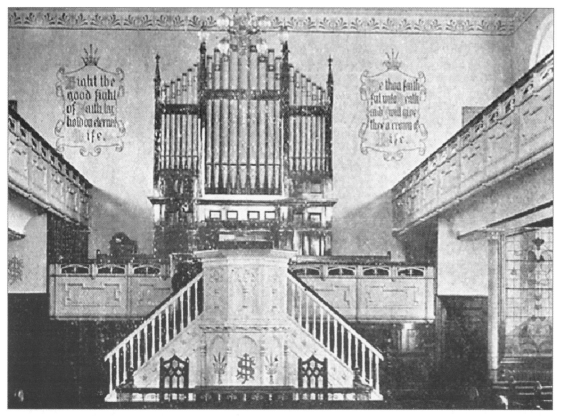

The interior of the New Connexion Methodist Chapel, on the opposite side of New Road to the Wesleyans. This picture comes from the front of the order of service, produced for the final service at this chapel on 23 October 1932. In a prompt reaction to Methodist Unification of that year, the New Connexion congregation had decided to close their chapel and 'cross the road'! It was built in 1838, and had last been renovated in 1905. *(Fran Davis)*

The Primitive Methodist chapel in Enville Street opened in 1857, with a foundation stone laid by Rowland Hill. Just to confuse everyone the congregation has met, in recent years, in the old Sunday school building in West Street, seen here in 2005. The small 'area for worship' was added on the right in 1968. *(David Howard)*

The little 'chapel' added to the West Street Sunday school was opened on 27 January 1969, but modesty has not saved it. The Enville Street (West Street) Chapel closed on 31 July 2005. *(David Howard)*

The Enville Street Ladies' Guild photographed in 1990. (David Howard)

The Enville Street Chapel's popular youth club was formed in 1945, and was led for many years by Dennis Howard, now a circuit steward. The club members appear on the stage at West Street, in this photograph of the late 1940s/early 1950s. A flourishing Amateur Dramatic Society grew out of activities at the chapel, which performed plays on this stage until the closure of the chapel in 2005. (David Howard)

Chapels that face closure often produce a final 'packed house'. On 17 July 2005 the hall at West Street was crammed with folks wanting to say goodbye to 'Enville Street'. They participated in an upbeat service celebrating the past and embracing future challenges. *(Ned Williams)*

After the farewell service at West Street on 17 July 2005 there was a photo call for the Youth Group (see photo on previous page). The decorations at the back recall the 1857–2005 history of the congregation, but even the Youth Group was able to celebrate sixty years of history. *(Ned Williams)*

The Particular Baptists established a congregation in Stourbridge in the 1820s, influenced and helped by colleagues at Brettell Lane. They built a chapel in Duke Street but remained small and prone to rifts. One rift, in 1829, led to a group erecting another chapel, which materialised in 1836 at Hanbury Hill. Celebrating the centenary of this congregation, W.T. Whitley produced a history of 'The Baptists in Stourbridge' in 1929. A photograph used in the 1929 publication looks much the same as this 2005 picture, but the rear of the building was much modernised in 1969. *(Ned Williams)*

The 1st Stourbridge Company of the Boys Brigade was founded at Hanbury Hill in 1975, and this photograph of the company was taken in 1984. *(175th Anniversary Collection)*

The Girls Brigade was established at Hanbury Hill in 1969 by Mrs D. Seeney. Here we see them parading through Gig Mill, School Street, in October 1979. *(175th Anniversary collection)*

The Reverend Marion Whittington (centre) and elders of Hanbury Hill Chapel stand in front of the history display, erected to help celebrate the chapel's 175th Anniversary on Wednesday, 10 November 2004. *(Ned Williams)*

10 Dudley

Dudley and Wolverhampton followed similar patterns of chapel development. In both towns the dissenters, in the form of the Congregationalists, built two chapels, which then competed to create offshoots. Meanwhile, the various Methodist factions erected large chapels close to the town centre, from which they could encourage other chapels to take root in the suburbs. In both towns the 'suburbs' were originally industrial communities. In Dudley's case it meant encouraging chapel building in Netherton, Kates Hill, Eve Hill and 'the Dock', just as the Wolverhampton chapels had to expand into Whitmore Reans, Blakenhall, and Horseley Fields. Twentieth- century suburbs were a different matter.

In this chapter 'Dudley' means the town, created as a Borough in 1865, with the boundaries that existed until the local government changes of 1966 (although the chapels of Netherton and Woodside received some coverage in *Black Country Chapels*).

The Old Meeting House in Dudley is well hidden, being approached through an entry from Wolverhampton Street. It is also partly obscured by its own Sunday school building, as indicated in this 2005 picture. The first Unitarian Meeting House in Dudley was erected in 1701 or 1702, and like all the others was destroyed in the Sacheverell riots of 1715, but rebuilt afterwards. The building underwent restoration in 1869 but now seems rather worse for wear. It is supported by a small congregation. *(Ned Williams)*

A drawing used in the 1906 Blocksidge Guide of the King Street Congregational building.

The world of the dissenters was facing a number of splits and disagreements in the 1780s, with new congregations constantly being formed. One such faction met in New Mill Street from 1788 onwards, but in 1839 they laid the foundation stones for this 'Congregational' building in King Street. It opened a year later and carried the 'Erected AD1840' legend until its demolition in the 1980s. It was an important chapel in Dudley and nurtured a number of prominent Dudley citizens, rivalled from 1878 onwards by Christ Church. In 1972 the congregation joined the United Reformed Church and was subsumed into the Trinity Road church. *(Dave Whyley)*

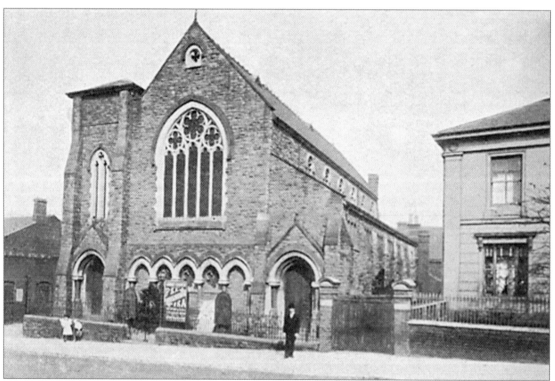

Christ Church, Waddams Pool, as illustrated in the 1902 Blocksidge Guide. It was decided to build a second Congregational chapel in Dudley in 1866 and a school building was erected in Fir Street to serve the Kates Hill population. Foundation stones for the chapel were laid on 28 August 1877 and it opened on 26 November 1878. The chapel was built by Nelson & Son of Dudley, and designed by the Wolverhampton architect, George Bidlake, in his church-like style (the tower originally supported a spire). *(Dave Whyley)*

The Presbyterian faction among the dissenters in Dudley laid the foundation stone for their chapel in January 1847 on a site in Wolverhampton Street, then on the outskirts of town!

The chapel, known by the Presbyterians as 'Trinity', to emphasise their differences with the Unitarians, was opened in November 1847.

The church was destroyed by a fire on 25 June 1944, and four years later construction of a 'church hall' began so the congregation could be accommodated pending completion of a proper place of worship.

This photograph was taken in 1868 and appeared in a local publication of that year. *(Dudley Archives & Local History Centre Collection)*

The foundation stone for the new 'Trinity', facing Trinity Road, was laid on 27 November 1948. A 'time capsule' was discovered soon afterwards, as demolition of the old church was completed. The building seen in this 2005 photograph was opened by Alfred Owen on Saturday 24 September 1949. *(Ned Williams)*

The two Congregational chapels established in Dudley, King Street and Christ Church, competed in many ways. In particular, they both nurtured missions in poorer areas. One interesting area in which everybody seemed keen to battle for souls was 'The Dock', consisting of 'The Old Dock', on the town side of Wellington Road, and 'The New Dock', on the country side of the road.

The Primitive Methodists built in Wellington Road itself. The Church of England opened a mission on the corner of Charlotte Street and Steppingstone Street in about 1880, in the heart of the Old Dock.

Meanwhile, the Christ Church 'Congs' opened the Lawley Street Mission in the New Dock, and the King Street 'Congs' supported a nearby mission in Maugham Street. The former was led by Thomas Amos, seen here in April 1906 cutting the first sod for a chapel that would replace both the Lawley Street and Maugham Street missions. *(Left and below: Doreen Amos collection)*

Thomas Amos (opposite page) was cutting the sod for the Park Congregational Chapel to be built at the foot of Grange Road. In the picture at the foot of the opposite page he is seen laying the foundation stones on 11 June 1906. On Wednesday 6 October of the same year the chapel, as seen in the 2005 picture above, was opened. It is an elegant red brick building of the straightforward style adopted by the less affluent chapels of that time (compare this with Stratton Street, Wolverhampton, page 127, also opened in 1906, and the Macefield Mission, Old Hill, of 1904).

The remarkable Mr Thomas Amos died in 1908 at the age of 62. He was replaced by J.T. Price, an equally remarkable man, who ran the Park Chapel for the next twenty-five years. During that time it was sometimes called 'Price's Mission' – not to be confused with the Price Street Mission of Kates Hill! A committee ran Park Chapel's affairs with representatives of Christ Church, King Street, and the County Union. Just before J.T. Price's death in 1933 it graduated from being a 'mission' to becoming an independent church with its own elected deacons. *(Ned Williams)*

The corridor at 'Park' features a whole row of foundation stones, seen being laid in the picture opposite. Both King Street and Christ Church are represented, then the County Union and the Dudley Free Church Council, the Netherton 'Congs' from Primrose Hill, these two stones from Lawley Street and the two stones laid by the men in top hats: James Smellie and F.W. Cook – well-known Dudley men. *(Ned Williams)*

During the 1930s Park Chapel issued a set of two postcards as a fund-raising idea. One showed the exterior of the building, this one showed the interior. The organ had been added in 1929 and at the same time the oak panelling was added to the walls. The organ cost £420, the panelling cost nearly £300. 'Park' did not join the United Reformed Church in 1972 and is therefore one of a number of local Congregational churches that have retained their independence. Apart from some new blue chairs and blue carpet, the interior is still like this today. *(Doreen Amos collection)*

The Congregationalists also expanded into Woodside and opened this little chapel, or 'Meeting House', in 1844. The picture was taken in 1974 just before its closure. It was built to face Woodside's 'High Street', now known as Highgate Road, and backed onto the pitbanks later reclaimed as a recreation ground and park. Woodside was well served by chapels: the New Connexion built 'Mount Zion' on the other side of Highgate Road, and the Wesleyans and 'Prims' were in Hall Street (now Hallchurch Road). All this activity reflected the importance of Woodside and Cochrane's Woodside Ironworks in the nineteenth century. *(K. Mole)*

The Dudley Baptists have a memorial stone in the foyer of this chapel informing us their history goes back to 1772. They first met in New Street, opening a chapel there in 1777. This building was opened on 24 September 1936 in Priory Road, still relatively close to the centre of Dudley. *(Ned Williams)*

Some elegant 1930s curves grace the interior of the Priory Road Baptist Church in Dudley, and the light oak pews contrast with the pastel shades of the plasterwork to create a light, airy ambience. Both photographs were taken in 2005. *(Ned Williams)*

The Wesleyan Methodists put on a big show in King Street, Dudley – rather in the same way the Darlington Street building was an impressive part of the Wolverhampton scene. John Wesley visited Dudley fifteen times and a 'preaching house' was established in the Mambles – a name borrowed by the Methodists in Coseley when they built their first chapel. When the Wesleyans outgrew this building in 1788 they built a chapel in King Street, then known as 'Back Lane'. The chapel went through several dramatic rebuilds and extensions, particularly in 1818 and 1904. When W.H. Cross wrote about the chapel in the 150th Anniversary booklet of 1938, he described the frontage as red brick with terracotta facings (presumably a result of the 1904 rebuild), set well back from the road, with an asphalted courtyard and handsome iron railings – as seen in this postcard view. The wing on the right, surmounted by a dome, was the caretaker's house! The wing on the left housed the ladies' parlour and Guild Room. *(Ken Rock collection)*

Opposite, below: The huge interior of the King Street Wesleyan Methodist Chapel, as illustrated in the 1938 brochure.

Below: An early 1950s Sunday school anniversary at King Street Methodist Chapel, Dudley, photographed from the balcony. *(Mabel Pearsall)*

Another Sunday school anniversary picture from King Street, this one taken in 1958, shows the children grouped round a model of the King Street premises, which compares well with the details of the building illustrated on page 83.

The Wesleyan circuit in Dudley eventually included Dixons Green and Salop Street, serving Dudley's inner suburbs of Kates Hill and Eve Hill respectively, and then beyond to Darby End, Netherton, Woodside, Upper Gornal, Gornal Wood, Pensnett, and Burnt Tree, on the fringe of Tipton. King Street's rival was not a Wesleyan chapel at all, it was the New Connexion in Wolverhampton Street, with which it was obliged to merge after a final service on 26 December 1965. (Mabel Pearsall)

The Wesleyan Methodist Chapel at Dixons Green as illustrated in the 1902 edition of Blocksidge's Guide. It was designed by Messrs Holton & Connor of Dewsbury, and built by Messrs Holland & Sons of Dudley. The foundation stone was laid on 2 August 1869 and the church was opened on Tuesday 16 August 1870. (Dave Whyley)

The interior of the 'old' Dixons Green Chapel, seen above, matched its Gothic exterior. This disappeared when the chapel was rebuilt. A new front was built incorporating the original foundation stone of 1869. The chapel was reopened in its modern form – as seen below – in 1950. A further rebuild took place in 2000. *(Ned Williams)*

The choir and Sunday school students celebrate the 130th Anniversary at Dixons Green on 22 May 2005, recalling that the Sunday school – originally accommodated behind the 1870 building – was opened in 1875. The theme for 2005 was 'Girls Who Made a Difference'. The Dixons Green Chapel has absorbed folks from Price Street and the 'Bethel', in Kates Hill and Burnt Tree. *(Ned Williams)*

A chapel calling itself 'The Methodist Free Church' was built in Kates Hill in 1867. Better known simply as the 'Bethel', it occupied a site at the junction of Brown Street and High Street, seemingly enjoying an independent existence. *(Peter Glews/D. Williamson)*

Salop Street Wesleyan Chapel
was the second Wesleyan
chapel to open in Dudley, but
it disappeared in the
rationalisations of the 1960s
and housing now occupies
the site. *(Joyce Round)*

A Sunday school anniversary photograph taken at Salop Street Methodist Chapel, *c.* 1950. *(Elsie Hadley)*

The Wesley Methodist Chapel, Wolverhampton Street, Dudley. *(Dudley Archives)*

In Dudley, where Top Church is 'low church' and Bottom Church is 'high church', we should not be surprised to find the Wesley Chapel was not Wesleyan for most of its life. It was 'New Connexion'! An explanation follows:

In 1828 the King Street congregation seemed keen to expand and bought the land near Wolverhampton Street on which the 'Wesley' was built. The foundation stone was laid on 10 June 1828, and it was opened just over a year later, on 16 August 1829.

Meanwhile, going back to 1821, the New Connexion Methodists had already become established in Dudley. At first they met in members' homes but eventually built a chapel, the 'Ebenezer', in Caddicks End (later named Chapel Street), which they used until 1845.

The congregation at the Wesley Chapel fell out with their fellow Wesleyans in 1835, uniting with the Methodists of the New Connexion. The 'wedding', as it was called, formerly took place on 29 August 1836. Thus Dudley's second Wesleyan chapel became a New Connexion chapel, one of about twenty New Connexion chapels to be found in the area at the time.

In 1865 the chapel had to be enlarged by pushing back the rear wall, and the chapel passed through a period of successive 'revivals', which added to its congregation. The Dudley circuit was one of the largest in the New Connexion, and played host to the Annual Conference in 1875, 1889, and 1903. The 1889 conference benefited from the arrival of electric light – the first chapel in Dudley to be so lit.

The New Connexion folks had established a Sunday school at their Ebenezer Chapel and then moved the school to a purpose-built place in Stafford Street. This fell out of use following the opening of Rose Hill Sunday school on 6 November 1859. The distinctive building had a grand entrance in Tinchbourne Street, occupying land at the rear of the Wesley Chapel.

The Wesley Chapel became 'Dudley Central' on 1 January 1966, when four Methodist congregations merged: Wesley, Wellington Road, Salop Street, and King Street. Later the Priory Methodists also became part of 'Central'.

At the time of the merger it was decided to build a new church. This took several years in the planning. The last service was held in the old 'Central' on 28 October 1973, but the building was not demolished until 1977, a service being held on the demolition site on 16 October of that year. The new church opened on 16 September 1978. The bricks from the 'old' Wesley were used to help rebuild 'Providence' in the Black Country Museum, and the organ from the old chapel was rebuilt and installed in the new one.

The Rose Hill Sunday school building of 1859 in Tinchbourne Street, at the back of the Wesley Chapel. The photograph was probably taken by Joe Round for use in the 1929 centenary booklet. *(Joyce Round)*

Another picture probably taken by Joe Round and used in the 1929 centenary booklet produced by the Wesley Chapel. Joe Round started training young people at Wesley Chapel in 1894. When he retired in 1957 he had served the chapel for sixty-three years. *(Joyce Round collection)*

Tom Gilpine, organist at the Wesley Chapel in Dudley for forty-eight years. He retired in 1979.

The organ was opened in May 1921 in memory of the fallen in the First World War. *(Joyce Round collection)*

Sunday school children and teachers pose for the camera at Wesley Chapel in 1959, when celebrating the centenary of the Sunday school building in Tinchbourne Street. *(Joyce Round collection)*

As is the case with many chapels, amateur dramatics flourished at the Wesley Chapel. Here we see a 1950s production performed in the large hall in the Tinchbourne Street building. The Rose Hill Dramatic Society was later known as the Central Players. *(Joyce Round collection)*

Dudley Central absorbed several congregations: Salop Street, Wellington Road and even King Street. When it absorbed the congregation of Laurel Road, in about 1973, it was in the process of planning a new building. Since the Methodists vacated Laurel Road, seen here in 2005, Pentecostal congregations have used the building. In 2005 it is known as 'Mount Olivet' and occupied by the First United Church of Jesus Christ Apostolic. *(Ned Williams)*

Laurel Road Methodist Chapel was built in the Priory Estate, on the corner of Laurel Road and Limepit Lane in 1938. Here we see the 11th Dudley Girl Guides on a Sunday school parade at Laurel Road, in about 1951. *(Jean Bullock)*

Vicar Street Methodist Chapel, Dudley, in 2005. This building dates from 1940 and replaced the Primitive Methodist Chapel built in 1902 on ground to the rear of this building. The 'campus' also included an institute building, where Bert Bissell's Men's Bible Class first met. *(Ned Williams)*

The 'Prims' in Dudley

The Primitive Methodists came to Dudley in 1818 from their stronghold in the Darlaston area. They enjoyed success in some of the poorer areas that others failed to reach. In Dudley that meant working in the Flood Street part of town. They built their first chapel in George Street in 1829.

They later opened another chapel in Wellington Road, but George Street remained top of a Dudley circuit that included chapels in Woodside and Netherton (Noah's Ark).

By the end of the nineteenth century George Street was dilapidated. It was sold and plans were drawn up to develop a site at the corner of Vicar Street and Martin Hill Street. The foundation stone was laid at Easter 1902 for the Sunday school building, which was completed and open by June of the same year. The adjacent chapel was built at the same time but presumably opened later. The latter was replaced in 1940.

The interior of the Vicar Street building of about 1902, sold as a postcard. This building stood behind the 1940 replacement until recent times but no exterior photograph of it has yet been found. *(Ken Rock)*

Bert Bissell's Young Men's Bible Class is Vicar Street's claim to fame. Although Bert Bissell became associated with leading young men to the summit of Ben Nevis, we see the Young Men's Bible Class here on a local outing at nearby Shaw Road, in 1928. Bert started the class as a young man in 1925. He is believed to be sitting behind the shield in this picture. Just below the Vicar Street flag is a large version of the YMBC badge, a small enamelled lapel version being proudly worn by members. *(Brian and Viv Turner)*

Bert Bissell (1902–98) photographed at his home in Selbourne Road, in front of a mural depicting his beloved Ben Nevis in October 1997. He first conquered the mountain in 1937, climbing it every year thereafter with groups of young men from Dudley. He became well known as a peace campaigner and was Dudley's first Probation Officer. He had a profound influence on many people's lives. *(Brian and Viv Turner)*

The Primitive Methodists in Dudley seem to fare better in Wellington Road, where they could minister to the population of the 'Old Dock'. The local congregation managed to build a plain chapel in Wellington Road in 1861, seen here in a drawing reproduced in Blocksidge's Guide. In 1869 over £1,000 was spent upgrading the chapel externally and internally to its more familiar form, seen below. *(Dudley Archives)*

In aid of
PRICE ST. MISSION
Sunday School Anniversary
July 7th, 1963

Price 2d.—Thank You !

Raistrick & Co. Ltd., 96, Harris Street, Bradford, 1.

SUNDAY SCHOOL ANNIVERSARY
BETHEL METHODIST CHURCH
KATESHILL, DUDLEY.

May 8th. 1960

THANK YOU

Phul-Nana Preparations can now be obtained from your local Chemist or Store.   Ask for lovely Phul-Nana Perfume, Face Powder, Lipstick, Rouge and Face Cream.
PHUL-NANA PERFUMERY, 54, NEASDEN LANE, LONDON.

Folks at Wellington Road, Dudley, pose outside the chapel after the 1950 anniversary service. On the left is the Minister, the Reverend George Underwood, and on his right, on the edge of the picture, is Sir Alfred Owen. Also present are Ben Fradgley, Sunday school superintendent, and Lewis Westwood, secretary. Other people seen here are members of the congregation at Central today, including Vera Hancox, who supplied the picture.

Wellington Road closed in December 1965 to amalgamate with Central. The chapel was later used as a Sikh gurdwara, for which purpose it has now been replaced by a more modern building. *(Vera Hancox)*

Sunday school 'tickets' collected by Doreen Amos.

St John's Church (1840), Kates Hill, fills the skyline of what may not seem to be a chapel photograph at all! However, this is Price Street in 1959, and on the right is the entrance to the Price Street Mission. The entrance to the mission itself was a sharp right turn, once through the entry; therefore the mission is rarely photographed, even in wedding scenes! The end wall is plain and is immediately adjacent to Edgar Westley's brass foundry. (*G.F. Homer/Dudley Archives*)

A Price Street Mission anniversary, *c.* 1950. Front left is Mr Westwood, superintendent; on the right is his daughter Mrs Newey, who taught the hymns. At the back, centre, is Mr Edward, organist. Among the children are Arthur and Margaret Fladgley, who provided the picture over fifty years later. (*A. & M. Fladgley*)

The present Salvation Army Hall in North Street, Waddams Pool, Dudley, was opened and dedicated on Saturday 29 September 1975 by Lieutenant Colonel N. Kirkwood. The hall is built on the site of Christ Church (see page 76). Before 1975 the Salvation Army Citadel was in King Street, in a building opened on 25 June 1932 by Dudley's MP: Dudley Joel. *(Ned Williams)*

Robert Merrick, photographed in May 2005, holds a picture of his grandfather, who was a Salvation Army soldier in Dudley in the 1880s. Family history is a strong thread to Army life.

The Salvation Army was established in Dudley by 1877 when the first meeting was held at the Temperance Hall, in the High Street, in the name of 'The Christian Mission'. A year later they moved to a chapel in Chapel Street, then to Bennett's old wooden theatre building in New Hall Street.

In 1901 General Booth came to the Dudley Opera House to address local 'soldiers', by which time the Dudley Corps was based in King Street. *(Ned Williams)*

Dudley's Salvation Army Band on the stage at the King Street Citadel, *c*. 1937. The bandmaster (centre) was Ted Jewkes, and the officers (either side of the stage) are Major and Mrs Stobart. They are wearing their 'Festival' tunics, worn during concert performances. *(Robert Merrick)*

The Dudley Salvation Army band in more recent times, at the North Street premises. The bandmaster is R. Hall. *(Robert Merrick)*

Dudley Salvation Army, The Young People's Band of 1921, seen at the King Street Hall. Front row, left to right: Charly Smith (grandfather of the present bandmaster), Don Plant, George Clayton, -?-, Jack Clayton, and Jack Reese. *(Ruth Round)*

The Young People's songsters, led by Ruth Round on the right, standing next to Horace Wilkinson, YP's Sergeant Major – a rank equivalent to that of school superintendent. *(Ruth Round)*

The Dudley Salvation Army Young People's 'Singing Company' of 1971. *(Robert Merrick)*

A sponsored 'play-in' by the Primary Group Band (Dudley Salvation Army) in November 1975. They raised £50 towards the new hall. In uniform, on the left, Pam Randall; on the right, Dianne Hale. The children are, back row, left to right: Julia Hale, Stephen Brookes, Martin Randall, Neil King, Colin Wilson, John Kitchen. Second row: Blaire King, Matthew King, Robert Cherrington, Alison Clouston, James Hale, and Stuart Randall. Front row: Alison Kitchen, Charlotte Coley, Lorraine Brookes, Richard Goodall and Patrick Smith. *(Dianne Hale collection)*

Julia Hale collecting money for the Dudley Salvation Army Band in 1967. *(Dianne Hale collection)*

The Salvation Army Songsters' photocall at the North Street Hall on 15 May 2005. *(John James)*

11 Upper Gornal

Upper Gornal lies halfway between Dudley and Sedgley, a complete community in itself. The parish church, St Peter's, dates back to 1838, and all the chapel denominations are represented, either in Upper Gornal itself or in nearby Ruiton.

Two congregations of interest, but not pictured here, are the Pentecostals of Eve Lane, and the Baptists in Jews Lane. The Pentecostal folks built their first 'Assemblies of God' chapel in Eve Lane back in 1938. In the 1970s they replaced it with a large modern building, reflecting their success in nurturing a congregation. In 1922 a breakaway group from the Robert Street Strict Baptists provided themselves with a small chapel at the top of Jews Lane. It took the name 'Rehoboth'.

In about 1974 the building became a Kingdom Hall for the Jehovah's Witnesses, but is currently used as a children's nursery.

In this chapter we will look at the two Methodist chapels in Upper Gornal that have amalgamated to create the present-day Methodist Church.

The Wesleyan Methodist Chapel in Kent Street, Upper Gornal, was built in 1832, and this photograph was taken in the 1900s while the tram tracks still occupied Kent Street. Although the frontage was brick, the side walls were local Gornal stone. *(Colin Hale)*

After the Methodist Unification of 1932 the 'AN' was removed from the frontage of the Kent Street chapel and it simply became 'The Wesley'. The brickwork has been rendered and the railings were replaced with a brick wall. The photograph was taken just before demolition in 1970. *(Colin Hale)*

Mount Zion Chapel, Kent Street, Upper Gornal. Mount Zion was only 250 yards away from the Wesleyan Chapel, but it was built by their rivals, the New Connexion Methodists, in 1878. *(Colin Hale)*

The interior of
Mount Zion just
before demolition
in the 1970s.
(Colin Hale)

One of the last anniversaries at Mount Zion. In the centre, left to right: George Greathead (choirmaster),
an unknown preacher, the Reverend Eddie Smith (Minister), and John Grainger (organist). *(Colin Hale)*

At Easter 1970 the two Methodist chapels in Upper Gornal amalgamated, and the Wesley congregation came to share the Mount Zion building for a time. On 15 July 1978 the new church opened, set well back from the main road, as seen in this 2005 photograph. The car park seen on the left marks the former site of Mount Zion. A little parcel of land in front of the Spills Meadow public house, plus the brick walls pictured two pages back, marks the location of the Wesley, and the burial chamber that was once beneath it. *(Ned Williams)*

The New Connexion seems to have been strong in the Gornals, with Mount Zion in Upper Gornal and the spectacular 'Zoar' in Gornal Wood (see *Black Country Chapels*, page 76). Another New Connexion chapel that slipped through the net in *Black Country Chapels* is this building at Ruiton Street, seen here in 2005, named 'Five Ways'. It dates from 1841 and three buildings are thought to have been joined to create the chapel, not entirely obliterated by modern extensions. *(Ned Williams)*

12 Coseley

In *Black Country Chapels* we covered one or two chapels in Coseley in Chapter 11, 'Through the villages'; while in the chapter on 'Missions' we looked at St Cuthberts as an Anglican 'Mission church', which seemed chapel-like. Now we return to Coseley to look at another pair of chapels, one Baptist, one Methodist.

Left: Baptists first established themselves in the Coseley/Bilston area at Darkhouse, at the end of the eighteenth century. From the Darkhouse Chapel, the Baptists established themselves in the Salem Chapel at Bilston (see page 133). In about 1805 a congregation was established in West Coseley, and in 1809 they built the first 'Providence' Chapel, seen here in what became known as Providence Row.
By the 1870s the congregation had outgrown this chapel and the widow of a late minister cut the sod that marked the start of work on its successor (see above), which was opened on 1 July 1871. This building became the church hall, subsequently improved (in 1877, for instance), but sadly later demolished. *(Elaine Ganston)*

Right: This drawing portrays the Providence Baptist Chapel of West Coseley, in its original form of the 1870s. The distinctive pinnacles were removed in 1958, and the building has undergone further rebuilding, but it remains an unusual looking chapel – as seen on the next page.
(Elaine Ganston)

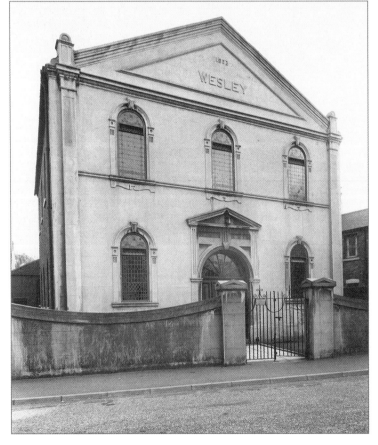

Coseley Providence Baptist Chapel in 2005. Lowered, and shorn of its pinnacles, the building still retains its distinctive porch. Like many chapels, it has had to defend itself from attacks by vandals, retreating behind this rather brutal grey fence. *(Ned Williams)*

The Wesleyan Methodists in Coseley first erected a building in Mamble Square, now the site of Coseley Baths. In the 1850s they decided to move to Bayer Street, Roseville. The first step was to use some of the materials from Mamble Square to build a Sunday school building, and then construction began of the new chapel. The building was opened on 17 July 1853.

The interior view of Roseville Chapel reveals a pulpit of great historical interest. It appears to have come from the old Wesleyan Chapel in Wheelers Fold, Wolverhampton ('Noah's Ark'). John Wesley himself may have preached from the pulpit in 1787. It was moved to Darlington Street in 1820 and then it was offered to the Mamble Square Trustees in 1851. Only the reading desk portion still exists. *(Both Roseville pictures supplied by Harold Westwood)*

The old Roseville Chapel closed on 7 October 1979 and on 8 March 1980 the congregation moved into a new chapel built as an extension to their modern church hall of 1972 vintage. *(Ned Williams)*

The front of the new Wallbrook Methodist Chapel in Edge Street, which opened in 1963 (the old Wallbrook Chapel had opened around 1839). The new building's commemorative stone was laid on 17 April 1963, reminding all that the congregation had previously met in the (New Connexion) Methodist Chapel in Chapel Street. *(Mr & Mrs Jones collection)*

This chapel underwent a revival in the early twentieth century. This 1920s picture shows two football teams: the single men versus the married men! By this time the New Connexion had become the United Methodists, hence 'UMFC'. *(Mr & Mrs Jones collection)*

A 1960 picture of the anniversary at the old Wallbrook Chapel, Coseley. On the left is Mr Gough, who had led the choir for many years. Bottom right is Caroline Jones, the granddaughter of W.H. Jones, who appears top right in the football team opposite. Caroline's father, Ray Jones, was a steward at Wallbrook for sixty years. Such was the continuity of chapel life. *(Mr & Mrs Jones collection)*

A 1980s anniversary at Wallbrook in the new (1963) chapel, using the stage that was usually curtained off when the hall was being used for worship. Although the Sunday school was over ninety strong in 1963, the congregation declined and Wallbrook closed on 14 October 2001. Houses now occupy the site. *(Mr & Mrs Jones collection)*

The 1999 façade of the Darkhouse Lane Baptist Chapel hides a long history. The Baptists at Darkhouse Lane, Coseley established themselves at the end of the eighteenth century, with the help of early Baptists at Brettell Lane. In 1809 a group from Darkhouse spawned the congregation at Providence, at the other end of Coseley. A Particular Baptist succession from the latter helped establish Ebenezer (below) and so on. *(Ned Williams)*

A drawing of Coseley's Ebenezer Baptist Chapel makes it look slightly more 'squat' than it really is (see *Black Country Chapels*, page 71). As stated above, it was built by a group that broke away from Providence in 1856, supported by local ironmasters. The chapel was opened in September 1858. *(W. Boyd)*

13 Wolverhampton

Most Black Country towns provided themselves with a chapel of each persuasion as the nineteenth century progressed, and a second chapel, or more, if the town grew sufficiently and prospered. In the cases of Wolverhampton and Dudley, the pattern is slightly different. In these places chapels sprang up in the town centres, witnessing suburban development in the wake of population growth. And with larger populations came possibilities for schisms, splits and breakaways, all adding to the number and diversity of chapels eventually built.

As was often the case, dissent began from within the walls of the Church of England. The 1662 Act of Uniformity led the Rector of St Peter's, John Reynolds, to defect and a dissenting congregation was established. In 1701 the dissenters built their first meeting house in Wolverhampton, in St John's Lane. In 1781 this became 'Unitarian', and a group of Trinitarian secessionists moved to a barn in Pountney's Fold. In 1782 these 'Congregationalists' built themselves a chapel in Grey Pea Walk, now known as Temple Street.

With Wolverhampton firmly on John Wesley's itinerary, the Nonconformists would also soon start chapel-building in the rapidly expanding town.

A faction of the Congregationalists from Pountneys' Fold built a chapel in Princess Street, completed by 1809. When they outgrew this building they began work on the corner of Queen Street. The new chapel, completed in 1813, is featured in this drawing, used in later printed histories of the Wolverhampton 'Congs'. By the 1860s they had outgrown this chapel and George Bidlake was asked to design a much more 'church-like' replacement.

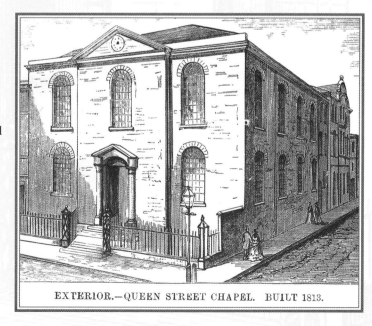

EXTERIOR.—QUEEN STREET CHAPEL. BUILT 1813.

George Bidlake designed an impressive home for the Congregationalists of Queen Street, costing £12,000. While it was being built they met in the Corn Exchange, eventually moving into their new premises on 9 January 1866.

The congregation included many influential Wulfrunians including Thomas Bantock and Samuel Manders, and the minister at the time – the Reverend T.G. Horton – became a well-known local figure.

The well-to-do members of the congregation financially supported the building of new missions and chapels. Samuel Mander was influential in the founding of Tettenhall College.

Queen Street closed towards the end of the 1960s and was demolished in 1970.

The pictures of the exterior and interior of the Queen Street chapel come from a centenary booklet produced by Henry May in 1909, one of several histories of local Congregationalism.
(Lawson Cartwright collection)

In the summer of 1845 there was a split in the congregation at Queen Street and a group broke away, establishing themselves at the Music Rooms in Cleveland Street. The Congregationalists joined them from Temple Street (see page 113) and they appointed a new minister, the Reverend W.H. Heudebourck. He inspired them with the vision of erecting a new building in the Gothic church style. Edward Banks drew plans for the church shown above, built in Snow Hill in the mid-1850s. By the time it was dedicated on 31 July 1849, Mr Heudebourck had already led another split! The introduction of more 'church-like' services caused further dissension. From the 1850s onwards, the two congregations at Queen Street and Snow Hill competed in the task of building more chapels. In 1941 the building depicted here partially collapsed but the congregation met in their church hall until 1964, when they joined the Penn congregation. *(Lawson Cartwright collection)*

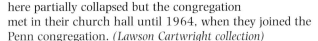

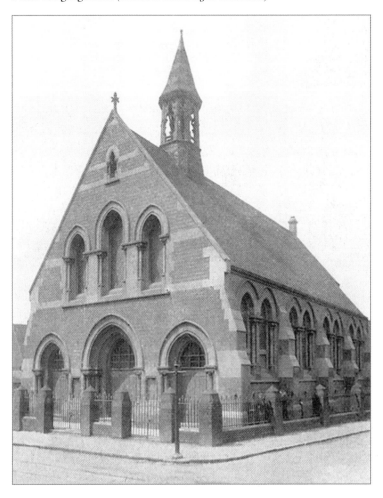

The Queen Street Congregationalists built this chapel in Heath Town, on the corner of Frederick Street and the Wolverhampton Road. It was designed by George Bidlake and opened on 14 July 1887. As long ago as 1839 the Temple Street dissenters had tried to establish themselves in Heath Town, establishing a chapel in Chapel Street. But in 1846 this building had to be leased to the Primitive Methodists, and was later used by the 'Free Gospellers'. *(Lawson Cartwright collection)*

Before heading for leafy suburbs, the Congregationalists at Queen Street wanted to promote chapels in the inner, industrial suburbs of Wolverhampton. A non-sectarian 'town mission' was established in 1855 and four years later Samuel Mander brought it within the orbit of the Congregationalists. In 1866 this chapel, or 'mission hall' as it says above the door, was built in York Street. It was able to seat 350 and for once George Bidlake was able to design something not 'church-like'! *(Lawson Cartwright collection)*

The Queen Street Congregationalists also turned their attention to Tettenhall, wishing to build in Strockwell Road, but they met opposition from the Church of England. In 1867 a congregation began to meet in a small chapel in Tettenhall Wood, built by the Wesleyan Methodists back in 1824. Once again, George Bidlake came along and designed them a church-like building, seen on the left. It was opened on 3 June 1873. The old Wesleyan chapel next door was turned into a Sunday school building.

The Congregationalists also looked further afield to Swindon, Wombourne, Shipley, and Wall Heath. *(Lawson Cartwright collection)*

The 'tin tabernacle' in Swan Bank, Penn, was opened in 1902, in what was then a village outside Wolverhampton. In 1966 it joined the newer and larger Penn Congregational Church on Penn Road. Houses now occupy the site. *(Reg Parnwell)*

The Snow Hill Congregationalists also planted other chapels. In 1867, for example, they opened a mission at Park Street, Blakenhall. Further afield they assisted chapels at Brewood and Wheaton Aston. After the Second World War it was decided that a chapel should be built in the new suburbs, in particular at Penn. Foundation stones were laid in 1950 and the building, seen here nearing completion, was opened on 6 December 1951. Church hall and side rooms were added in 1964. Six years after absorbing the congregations from Swan Ban, Snow Hill, and Park Street, they became part of the United Reformed Church in 1972. *(Lawson Cartwright collection)*

The Congregationalists at Queen Street, and Alderman Bantock in particular, did all they could to help establish a new Congregational chapel in Lea Road, Penn Fields. The chapel featured on the cover of *Black Country Chapels* and the pictures on pages 52 and 53 show the results. Here we see foundation stones being laid on 11 July 1931 for the building opened in 1932. In the white dress is Joy Cooksey, who was held over the trench by her mother to lay the second stone. In July 2005 Joy returned to celebrate the congregation's centenary.

Below: In 1996 the foundations of the new building, opened 24 February 1966, had been laid, and members gathered to inspect progress, led by Joan Jones (church secretary) in hard hat. Note the same houses feature in the background of both photos. *(Anne Peters)*

Methodism in Wolverhampton can trace its origins to John Wesley's first visit to the town in 1753. In 1787 Wesley himself was able to open a Meeting House in Wheelers Fold, off Lichfield Street, at the back of the Noah's Ark Inn. In 1824 this building was sold and the Wesleyans built a new chapel on the outskirts of the town, in a new thoroughfare, called Darlington Street. It opened on 26 August 1825, with room enough for 800 people. It was enlarged in 1860 in the form illustrated here. Then in 1901 it was enlarged yet again to its present form: the Methodist 'cathedral' of the Black Country. In the 1860s Wesleyan chapels were built in the suburbs of Whitmore Reans and Compton Road. 'Trinity', on Compton Road and Darlington Street became the centres of two circuits. *(Darlington Street Church Archives)*

Eminent Wulfrunians were also associated with Methodism and helped promote its expansion. Mrs Thorneycroft (wife of Wolverhampton's first Mayor), John Hartley, and his nephew Henry Fowler (Later Lord Wolverhampton), promoted 'Trinity' on the Compton Road, not far from Chapel Ash. John Hartley laid the foundation stone on 6 October 1862, and it was dedicated on 30 June 1863. It was designed by George Bidlake. In 1888 it became head of the circuit created on the western side of Wolverhampton. *(David Clare)*

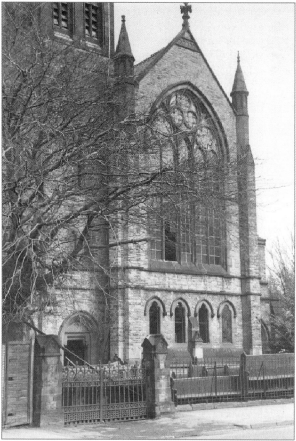

The interior of 'Trinity', Compton Road, showing the chancel window provided by Henry Fowler (Lord Wolverhampton), Wolverhampton MP, and the first Methodist to sit in the Cabinet, and later, the House of Lords. The Trinity circuit included Coven, Brewood, Penn Road (of 1878), Newhampton Road (of 1885), the Merridale Street Mission (of 1900), and the chapel at Bradmore: the latter ultimately transforming itself into the church at Beckminster. From the choir came the Trinity Operatic Society, which still exists today. 'Trinity' closed in 1973 and flats now occupy the site. *(David Howard)*

The Wesleyan Chapel in Whitmore Reans was built in Newhampton Road West in 1885. Today it is replaced by the ultra-modern Cranmer Methodist Church. *(David Clare)*

Beckminster Methodist Church, photographed in 2005, carries the date 1926 above its door. Its history goes back to the unification of two Wesleyan congregations: Penn Road and Bradmore, both at one time part of the Trinity circuit. Penn Road began in a wooden building, replaced by a chapel in Mander Street in 1877. It later reoriented itself towards the Penn Road – hence the name. The Bradmore congregation began in a local smithy, and in 1907 moved into a chapel built at the Bradmore crossroads. Today the building is a community centre. In 1923 the two congregations were amalgamated and moved to a new church on the Beckminster Estate. It was designed by Messrs Crouch, Butler and Savage, and built by S.F. Swift & Sons, at a cost of £14,000. It opened in 1926. *(Ned Williams)*

Springdale Methodist Church when new in 1953. *(Geoff Race)*

The interior of Springdale Methodist Church today. The exterior, as in 1953, is seen on the previous page. The congregation began to form in 1936, meeting at various locations, including the Penn Cinema (1938–40). The present site on Warstones Road was acquired in 1951 and A.M. Griffiths set out to build the chapel for £11,397. The building was opened on 24 October 1953. As seen here, the worship area has been completely turned round and the altar now stands in the former entrance. *(Ned Williams)*

Members of the Springdale Sunday school photographed on 5 June 2005, with banners once used on parades. Behind them is a quilt produced in 2003 to mark the 50th birthday of the church. Local churches now work together as 'Churches in Penn': Springdale and Beckminster Methodists, Penn Road UR, and local Roman Catholics. *(Ned Williams)*

The Wesleyan Methodist chapels on the eastern side of Wolverhampton do not seem to be so well photographed. Here we resort to a wedding picture to portray the Heath Town Wesleyan Methodist Chapel – even then the photographer had to step into the middle of the main Wolverhampton Road to record the marriage of Stan to Janet Barnard on 29 March 1958. This was another church designed by George Bidlake, opening in March 1860, and closing in 1963. *(Philip Barnard)*

The youth club Nativity play at Heath Town Wesleyan chapel, *c.* 1950. Janet Barnard, who appears on the far left, supplied the picture, and Betty Hopwood, third from the left, can still name all the participants in what was apparently an avant-garde production for its day! *(Philip Barnard)*

The Wesleyans at Darlington Street established an early outpost at Wednesfield. This chapel was built in Rookery Street in 1825. In March 1887 the congregation transferred to the new 'Trinity' chapel. The latter was demolished in 1984. Meanwhile, the Rookery Street building enjoyed a long and varied career. For many years it was 'The Ideal' cinema, known locally as 'The Smack'. When this picture was taken in 1982 it had become a carpet warehouse. Later it was victim of a fire. *(Ned Williams)*

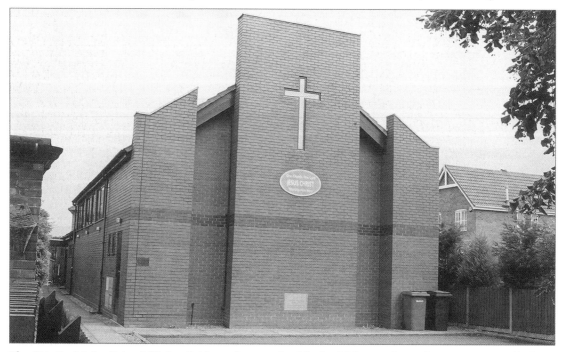

The Trinity Methodists of Wednesfield amalgamated with the Hickman Street (ex-Primitive Methodists) in 1964, and in 1983 moved to this new centre at Wood End. *(Ned Williams)*

The New Connexion Methodists missioned Wolverhampton in 1810, eventually building a chapel in Horseley Fields in 1829. It was always known as 'Mount Zion'. It was rebuilt in 1867 and became the centre of a small New Connexion circuit. By the end of the century there were four chapels in the circuit: one at Church Street, Heath Town, one at Moseley Village (Near Deans Road), and one at Froysell Street, Willenhall. When this picture was taken, in the 1970s, it was surviving as the Guru Ravidas Sikh temple, having been abandoned by the Methodists in 1968. In the early 1980s it was demolished. *(David Clare)*

The lofty interior of Mount Zion Chapel in Horseley Fields was impressive, but its congregation rapidly declined as many houses in the area were demolished and the new ring-road ran through that part of Wolverhampton. *(Judy Booth collection)*

In 1878 a local preacher called George Cope tried to persuade the New Connexion to take over an abandoned Wesleyan mission in Heath Town. When his plea was rejected he established an independent congregation in Heath Town, in a house in Prestwood Road. In 1881 the congregation moved to some cottages in Church Street – premises that became known as 'Cope's Chapel'. In 1908, four years after Cope's death, there was another move to 'Bethesda' in Thorneycroft Road. The final move came on 22 October 1936, when this 'hacienda' style building was opened in Wimbourne Road, Fallings Park. The architect was Frank Birch. *(Ned Williams)*

Primitive Methodist missionaries descended on the Wolverhampton area in 1819 but had more success in surrounding towns than in Wolverhampton itself. They conducted open-air meetings in the style of John Wesley, often meeting with opposition. Their first local chapel was built in Lord Street in 1833.
A more impressive building was the 'Bethel' on the Dudley Road, in Blakenhall, seen here in 1977.
The congregation of this chapel are now to be found at St Johns, Parkfield.
(David Clare)

When Methodist Unification took place in 1932 there were forty-three chapels in Wolverhampton, belonging to the three principal branches of Methodism. It can be no surprise that many of these have now vanished. In January 1974 the 'Bethesda' Primitive Methodist Chapel was still standing in Waterloo Road, just beyond the junction with Stavely Road. It appears to have opened in 1880 and closed in 1966. *(David Clare)*

'Primitive Methodist 1906', is proudly proclaimed across the gable-end of the Stratton Street Chapel, Park Village, and the row of foundation stones just below window-level are dated 1 October 1906. Amazingly it survives in 2005. *(Ned Williams)*

The Wolverhampton Salvation Army Citadel in Cleveland Road, *c.* 1974. This is a handsome building in the style popular at the turn of the twentieth century. The Corps has since moved to more modest premises on the Willenhall Road. *(Ned Williams)*

Representatives of the Wolverhampton Corps of the Salvation Army assemble outside the Wolverhampton Civic Centre on 16 June 2002, to take part in the Civic Sunday Parade. Left to right: Jean Head, John Head, Captain Geoff Bonsor, Peter Armstrong, Captain Glenys Bonsor, June Armstrong, and her grandson, Lee. *(Ned Williams)*

The Wolverhampton Salvation Army Band at Cleveland Road, *c*. 1966. In the centre is bandmaster, Charlie Handwell, flanked by Lieutenants Mr and Mrs Turner, who led the Corps at the time. *(Jean Head Collection)*

The one-time Salvation Army Citadel in Cleveland Street is now Wolverhampton home to a congregation of the Mount Bethel African Methodist Episcopalian Zion Church, also to be found at George Street, Bilston (see *Black Country Chapels*, page 63). This photograph was taken on 14 July 2002. *(Ned Williams)*

Hymn singing outside the Assemblies of God Pentecostal Church in Temple Street, April 1953. The church was established by sisters Elsie & Jennie Wood in 1941. This distinctive doorway is now, in 2005, the entrance to the Church of All Nations. *(Express & Star)*

Awaiting the opening of the New Testament Church of God in Nursery Street, Wolverhampton, on Saturday 27 January 1962. *(Express & Star)*

The Westbury Chapel at the junction of Broad Street and Westbury Street was officially opened on 21 July 1962, but the congregation has a longer history. Members first gathered in Clarence Street in 1885 as the 'Open Brethren' but later moved to an ex-Methodist chapel in Cleveland Street, where there is now an entrance to the Mander Centre. They left Cleveland Street in about 1960 and acquired the site now used in Westbury Street, which survives as an independent free evangelical chapel. This picture shows the Broad Street entrance to a centre in front of the main chapel. On the left, beneath the trees, is a Quaker burial ground. *(Ned Williams)*

The chapel beside Wolverhampton's West Park began life as 'All Souls' built by the Unitarians to replace a chapel in Bath Road. Planned early in 1911 by J.L. Ball, Henry Lovatt and the local builder completed it ready for an opening on 16 November of the same year. In recent years it has been used by a successful independent evangelical congregation and the Unitarians gather in the nearby Quaker Meeting House. *(Ned Williams)*

The Penn Christian Centre, Warstones Road, Spring Hill, opened on 17 November 1985. It began with a small congregation, which has gone from strength to strength. But the building has a longer history. A group from the Cleveland Street Gospel Hall bought the plot in the 1930s and built a small hall (known as Cleveland Hall), which probably opened just before the war. The group sometimes flourished and sometimes floundered, and passed the hall on to a second group. This congregation had virtually abandoned the place by the time the Christian Centre took over in 1985. This independent evangelical group has extended the hall forwards, as can be seen in the photograph, and given it a more modern appearance. *(Ned Williams)*

The chapel in Cleveland Street, from which folks migrated to Warstones Road (above) and to Westbury Street (see previous page), is something of a mystery, although it is clearly marked on some old maps. This drawing of it was later reproduced on the back of a Westbury Chapel publication in 1985. It seems to have disappeared in pushing an entrance through to the Mander Centre. *(Les Ford)*

14 Back to Bilston

The chapter on Bilston in *Black Country Chapels* almost exclusively concentrated on the Methodist chapels of the area. We return in this section to look at one Baptist and one Congregational Chapel, both of which survive today in new buildings, in new locations.

These two paintings by Edwin Millard hang in the vestry of the present-day Bilston Baptist Church in Prouds Lane, to remind folks of the congregation's previous existence at Wood Street. Some Baptists from Darkhouse came to the rescue of a struggling independent congregation in Wood Street, Bilston, in about 1800 and 'Salem' was born. It was much rebuilt in about 1860, presumably as seen here in Mr Millard's picture.

By the 1950s 'Salem' was ageing and the Council were interested in demolishing the building to make way for the redevelopment of the centre of Bilston. There were delays and Bilston had become part of Wolverhampton by the time last communion was held at Wood Street on 15 June 1972, the chapel's 172nd Anniversary. *(Elaine Gamston)*

The 11th Wolverhampton Company of the Girls Life Brigade was formed at 'Salem' in 1930, and this photograph was taken soon afterwards with George Allcock, Chaplain to the GLB and chapel secretary, standing centrally behind Miss Hilda Southwick – first GLB Captain, and later first woman deacon at the chapel. The company at the chapel today is the 1st Bilston Girls Brigade. *(Elaine Gamston)*

Salem anniversary 1941: the lad all alone in the second row is Timothy Jenkins, the Minister's son. On his left is six-year-old Sylvia Timms, who refused to appear on the platform unless she could sing a duet with Timothy! On Sylvia's left is Molly Sylvester, née Howell, who is still at the church today. *(Sylvia Horton collection)*

The new Bilston Baptist Church in Prouds Lane was opened on 18 July 1972, having been designed by Tom Hood, and built by H. Fidler of Wolverhampton. The name 'Salem' was dropped. *(Ned Williams)*

Portway Road Congregational Church replaced a building in Oxford Street in the 1960s. *(Ken Rodgers)*

Traditions are preserved at the Portway Congregational Chapel's Sunday school, including parading with a banner, and the annual Nativity play, both photographed during 2004. *(Ken Rodgers)*

15 Bethel Revisited

When the Bethel Chapel, Garrett Street, Harts Hill, was featured in *Black Country Chapels*, it brought a swift response from Winnie Emery of Dudley Wood. Winnie wanted to point out that the building shown on page 14 of *Black Country Chapels* was used as a Sunday school in her day and that the chapel itself was a corrugated iron structure erected in front of the brick building.

Just a reminder: The Bethel, Harts Hill, as it exists today. A New Connexion chapel of the Methodist New Connexion built in the 1850s and closed in 1963. However, Winnie Emery takes us back to the days when a 'tin tabernacle' stood in front of this building. Winnie and her family were much associated with the chapel. *(Ned Williams)*

Winnie Woodcock marries Fred Emery at the 'tin tabernacle' – the 'Bethel', Harts Hill, on 14 July 1951, photographed before proceeding to the reception in the brick building.

Winnie has been able to supply a rare photograph – a wedding taking place in a tin tabernacle! The Reverend Fred Hunt marries Winnie and Fred at the Bethel on 14 July 1951. Details such as the wooden panelling and the anniversary platform, still in place on the left, add to the interest. The legend over the arch above the organ declared: 'Praise to the Holiest in the Height'.

Winnie's archive of the Bethel Chapel includes an anniversary poster dating from 1951, in which her name appears as the speaker to the Sunday schoolchildren. *(Ned Williams)*

The football club associated with the Bethel Chapel was known as Harts Hill United. By 1914/15 when this picture was taken the New Connexion had become the 'United Methodists'. Jack Grainger, sitting behind the ball was captain, but was killed soon afterwards in the First World War. Top left is Harold Whorton who became Sunday school superintendent and a real stalwart of the chapel. On Jack Grainger's left is Ike Woodcock – Winnie Emery's father. *(Winnie Emery)*

The Harts Hill's Men's Class, seen here in the 1930s, included many of the young men in the football team! *(Winnie Emery)*

The Bethel was competitive, whether on the football field or in musical activities. On the left is Joseph Lewis the choirmaster. On the right, Mrs Amy Owen (Joseph's cousin), who taught elocution, plus four lads and Winnie Woodcock – members of the Inter-Sunday School Music and Elocution Competition team. *(Winnie Emery)*

The Bethel Choir takes the stage at Dudley Town Hall at a chapel choir competition in the 1930s. *(Winnie Emery)*

16 Lost Chapels

W hen chapels close they can suffer one of three fates: they can be purchased by a new congregation wishing to maintain them as a place of worship, they can be converted to some new use altogether, or they can vanish without trace.

Conversions

There has been a long established tradition of putting ex-chapels to new uses. Chapels in Railway Street, Horseley Heath, and New Hall Street, Princes End, and in Tansey Green, Pensnett, became cinemas just before the First World War. More recently, the Spring Street Chapel in Langley has become a theatre (see page 32). Frequently they become factories or warehouses, such as the Bethel, Harts Hill (see page 137), or more recently, Mount Tabor, Woodsetton. In recent times there has been more interest in converting them to domestic use.

The Waterfall Lane Mission, between Old Hill and Blackheath, was selling beds when photographed in June 2004. The Grange Road Mission had its roots here. (See *Black Country Chapels*, page 36)

Hayes Lane Chapel is now home to the Lye Amateur Boxing Centre. *(Ned Williams)*

The ex-Methodist chapel in Malt Mill Lane, Blackheath, seen here in 2004, has been turned into apartments. *(Ned Williams)*

The tiny ex-chapel in Fir Street at the appropriately named Gospel End, near Sedgley, seems to be disappearing into the undergrowth in 2005. It opened in 1846 as a Wesleyan chapel. *(Ned Williams)*

Vanished without trace . . .

In some parts of the Black Country large numbers of chapels have simply 'vanished'. The Alan Godfrey maps – published recently but showing the Black Country as it was in about 1900 – reveal the existence of all sorts of intriguing one-time chapels. Sometimes a wall or a vacant space will prove once to have housed a chapel, such as the wall and lawn at Spills Meadow, Upper Gornal, that guards a burial ground: once part of the Wesleyan chapel that stood on the site.

Anyone driving along Mount Pleasant, Quarry Bank, might notice a brick wall and brick gateposts outside the house next to Talbot Lane. This is nearly all that exists today to remind us of the Mount Pleasant New Connexion Chapel. It is already so forgotten that no one seems certain when it closed: although a few folks remember it being derelict in the 1950s, prior to demolition. But a glance at the Alan Godfrey map proves it did once exist! And just to confuse everyone, some maps show another little chapel – 'The Bethany' – down Talbot Lane: a chapel-hunter's challenge!

After a long and desperate search for a photograph and history of the Mount Pleasant Chapel, all we have to show are a key and a picture of the football team!

The key, seen on the right, was presented to Mrs S. Cartwright, the oldest member of the congregation, on 12 August 1925, when she reopened the church. The building had lain in a derelict condition for eighteen years, as a result of subsidence, while the congregation met in a Sunday school, contemplating, no doubt, the rebuilding of their chapel. Yet during that period it is evident the football team kept going, as seen in this picture from about 1921.

Meanwhile, we know neither the date of its original opening, nor final closure! *(William Cartwright)*

ACKNOWLEDGEMENTS

This book could not have been written without the considerable help of many people. I wish to thank all those who have corresponded with me, or who have made me welcome in their chapel or in their home, and who have been generous with their time and the resources they have made available.

In particular I wish to thank the following:

Geoff Allman, Doreen Amos, Jean Attwood, Andrew Bagnall, Janice Bartley, Geoff Beard, John Beckett, Colin Bellamy, Judith Booth, Eric Bowater, Enid Bridgwater, Eileen Brittain, Irene Brittain, Roland Burrows, Bill Cartwright, Lawson Cartwright, David Clare, Betty Clarke, Pamela Cleobury, Wendy & Tony Collins, David Copper, Terry Daniels, Fran Davis, John Disley, Liz Dooley, David Eades, Fred & Winnie Emery, Molly Fanthom, Les Ford, Arthur & Margaret Froggatt, Dorothy Goodall, Sylvia Green, Robert & Barbara Evans, Elaine Gamston, Peter Glews, Miriam Golden, Derek Hadley, the Reverend Headley, Colin Hale, Dianne Hale, Pauline Heath, Stan Hill, Keith Hodgkins, Sylvia Horton, Dennis & David Howard, Major John Howarth, John Hughes, John James, Alan Johnson, Mr & Mrs Ray Jones, John Lenton, Trevor Lowe, David Merrick, Mrs Mole, the Reverend Cat Morrison, Betty Nash, Reg Parnwell, Brian Payton, Mabel Pearsall, Martin Pearson, Iris Pegg, Anne Peters, Sylvia Pugh, Irewyn Peters, Ruth Pritchard, Geoff Race, Val Read, Mavis Rew, Joyce Round, Ruth Round, Keith Sammonds, Vera Round, Bernard Shaw, Kenneth Tibbbets, Colin Turton, Viv & Brian Turner, Harold Westwood, Richard Westwood, the Reverend Marion Whittington, Dave Whyley, Mrs D. Williamson, Sheila Wootton, Mervyn Wright. I am grateful to have received assistance from two historians of local Methodism: John Lenton in Wolverhampton and Geoff Beard in Smethwick.

Special thanks also, to Ken Rock, who made his postcard collection available and introduced me to 'Picturesque Oldbury'. The Archives at Dudley and Wolverhampton, and the editor of the *Express & Star*. Photoprocessors at Movie Magic (Coseley) and Juliet Thompson for photo restoration work. And to people who assisted in compiling *Black Country Chapels*, and whose help has been ongoing. Terri Baker-Mills has acted as my coordinator in relation to my 'work-life balance', and accompanied me to many chapels.

Photographic credit is given in each caption, and all reasonable effort made to acknowledge the source of a photograph correctly. The author is happy to make suitable redress in situations where someone claims ownership of a photograph after publication. This is one of those topics that never ends, and the author is happy to receive new information on the subject at any time.